PRESCHOOL DIRECTOR'S SURVIVAL GUIDE

135 Forms, Checklists, Letters, and Guidelines for Day-to-Day Management

Rebecca Graff

The Center for Applied Research in Education
West Nyack, New York 10995

10 9 8 7 6 5 4 3 2

Printed in the United States of America

Library of Congress Cataloging-in-Publication Data

Graff, Rebecca, [date]
    Preschool director's survival guide : 135 forms, checklists,
letters, and guidelines for day-to-day management / Rebecca Graff.
      p.   cm.
    ISBN 0-87628-619-8
    1. Education, Preschool—Handbooks, manuals, etc. 2. Nursery
schools—Administration—Handbooks, manuals, etc. 3. Education,
Preschool—Forms. I. Title.
LB2822.7.G73 1990
372.21—dc20   89-29666
                                                CIP

THE CENTER FOR APPLIED
RESEARCH IN EDUCATION
BUSINESS & PROFESSIONAL DIVISION
A division of Simon & Schuster
West Nyack, New York 10995

DEDICATION

To my husband Roy, who taught me to compute,
to my sons Ben and Chris, I couldn't have done this without you.
And to my friend Sue, who taught me that I can do it too, thank you.

ACKNOWLEDGEMENTS

Credit is due Community Nursery School in Sheridan, Wyoming, and Busy Bee Nursery in Windom, Minnesota, for allowing me to use the forms which were written for their programs.

Computer graphics in Forms 2–23, 4–10, and 10–1 were designed using *The Print Shop*®. Published with permission from Broderbund Software.

Business card printed courtesy of Noah's Ark Preschool in Sheridan Wyoming.

Artwork on the Publicity Flyer by Christopher William Graff.

ABOUT THE AUTHOR

REBECCA GRAFF, M.S., is currently an Assistant Director of Financial Aid at Mankato State University in Minnesota. The 13-year span of her career in early childhood education encompassed a variety of programs. She taught in Montessori schools and preschools, directed in day care centers and preschools, and founded a day care center. Her interests in education, program organization, and compliance with regulations led her to her new career in student services on a university campus.

ABOUT THIS SURVIVAL GUIDE

The purpose of this book is to help you run your preschool as efficiently as possible. If it is going to survive and prosper, to continue doing its exciting work with children, it must be run in a businesslike manner. And, like any other educational institution, a preschool needs a firm foundation in philosophy, policy, procedure, and organization upon which to build its personnel, clientele, and services. *Preschool Director's Survival Guide* will help you organize and operate your preschool most effectively so that you can get on with your work with children and their families. Although the title indicates that it is for Directors, this resource will also be useful to teachers, aides, support staff, administrators, members of governing boards, and home day care providers.

Whatever the size of your school or the nature of your early childhood program, there are forms and examples in this book to help you. Some forms, such as "Staffing Patterns" in Section 7, are presented in a number of different ways to accommodate various types and sizes of programs; you can choose the one most appropriate for use. Some forms are geared specifically for one type of program, such as "Licensed Capacity" in Section 7, which is designed for a home day care provider. In contrast, the "Class Checkout Chart" in Section 6 is geared for a large day care center. If a form does not suit your purposes, you can tailor it to fit your needs.

Materials in the *Guide* feature two formats, FORMS and EXAMPLES. The forms can be reproduced and used as is. Their function is data collection or record keeping. The examples provide the essential information that should be included in a given form or document. A sample of what the finished product might look like is then shown. For instance, Section 1 includes a "Bylaws Outline" followed by "Sample Bylaws." This is where your creativity takes over and you design your own documents based upon the guidelines given.

The Contents provides a complete listing of the 135 forms included in the *Guide.* For quick access and easy use, they are organized into ten sections, each focusing on a different aspect of preschool management:

Section 1, *Formal Structure,* will help you start a new program from conception to opening the doors. Included are samples of organizational documents and policies.

Section 2 contains *Personnel Forms* including job descriptions for administrative, teaching, and support staff. There are forms to help with hiring and firing, and forms to document continuing education.

Section 3 consists of *Registration Materials,* from registration forms to permission and release forms. Also included is a sample of an information booklet for parents.

Section 4 deals with *Parent-Teacher Conferences.* There are forms to send home to parents for conference appointments, along with suggestions for you to keep in mind when meeting with parents. Two assessments are included here: one for progress during the normal preschool year, and one for readiness for kindergarten.

Section 5 contains numerous forms to help you with *Curriculum Planning,* from long- and short-term goals to a daily schedule. Different types of calendars are included to help you organize those plans and goals into workable units.

Section 6 is a special section devoted to *Field Trips.* It contains permission forms, sample letters of request and thank you, and forms to document who has gone where, and when they will return.

Section 7, *Daily Record Keeping,* contains staffing patterns, attendance forms, and health and safety forms.

Section 8 includes two types of *Financial Forms,* one set related to tuition and payment of fees, and the other used in the preparation of financial reports and budget projections.

Section 9 provides *Advertising Samples,* from newspaper ads to t-shirts with the preschool's logo.

Section 10 is a collection of *Administrative Forms* including equipment inventories, order forms, and service and maintenance forms. The final form in this section is a preschool evaluation form to be completed by parents at the end of the year.

In compiling the samples used in this collection, I drew upon numerous sources—nursery schools, preschools, day care centers, and home providers. These examples are not intended to tell you how to run your program, but rather to offer suggestions to help organize record keeping and documentation. I hope these management tools will enable you to devote more time and energy directly to children.

Rebecca Graff

CONTENTS

SECTION 1 *Formal Structure* 1

Initial Organization

1–1   Starting a New Program 3
1–2   Articles of Incorporation Outline 5
1–3   Sample Articles of Incorporation 6
1–4   Bylaws Outline 8
1–5   Sample Bylaws 10

Policies

1–6   Personnel Policies Outline 15
1–7   Sample Personnel Policies 16
1–8   Program Policies Outline 20
1–9   Sample Program Policies 21
1–10   Safety and Health Policies Outline 24
1–11   Sample Safety and Health Policies 25

SECTION 2 *Personnel Forms* 30

Application Forms

2–1   Application for Employment 33
2–2   Personnel Attitudes Survey 35
2–3   Interview Rating Form 37
2–4   Reference Cover Letter 38
2–5   Reference Information 39

Job Descriptions

2–6   Director 40
2–7   Teacher 42
2–8   Teacher's Aide 43
2–9   Substitute Teacher 44

2–10   Secretary.. 45
2–11   Bookkeeper 46
2–12   Cook 47
2–13   Bus Driver 48
2–14   Maintenance/Housekeeping 49
2–15   Responsibilities of the Board of Directors............. 50
2–16   Parental Responsibilities 51

Employment Forms

2–17   Contract for Employment 52
2–18   Employee Time Sheet 53
2–19   Substitute Time Sheet................................. 54
2–20   Request for Leave 55
2–21   Criteria for Self-Evaluation of Program 56
2–22   Staff Evaluation...................................... 58
2–23   Letter of Reference 60
2–24   Award for Excellence 62
2–25   Employee Complaint 63
2–26   Documentation of Employment Problem................ 64
2–27   Supervisor/Staff Conference 65

Continuing Education Forms

2–28   Certificate of Training 66
2–29   Record of Continuing Education 67
2–30   Evaluation of Training 68
2–31   Voucher for Travel Expenses 69

SECTION 3   *Registration Materials* 70

3–1   Sample Procedure for Registration Meeting........... 72
3–2   Registration Checklist................................ 73
3–3   Sample Registration Letter 74
3–4   Preregistration Form.................................. 75
3–5   Parent Information Booklet Outline 76
3–6   Sample Parent Information Booklet 77
3–7   Registration Form 82
3–8   Enrollment Form for Child With Special Needs 84
3–9   Permission for Health Care 85
3–10   Field Trip Permission Form 86
3–11   Sample Parent's Page 87
3–12   Permission for Screening 88
3–13   Dental Card 89
3–14   Sample Calendar of Holidays 90
3–15   Sample Preschool Calendar 91

SECTION 4   *Parent-Teacher Conferences* 92

4–1   Suggestions for Conferences 94
4–2   Parent-Teacher Conferences 95

4–3   Conference Confirmation 96
4–4   All About Me 97
4–5   Kindergarten Entrance Skills 98
4–6   Individualized Plan for Child With Special Needs 100
4–7   Documentation of Concern for a Child 101
4–8   Child Concern Letter.. 102
4–9   Permission for Further Evaluation 103
4–10   Child Award.. 104
4–11   Record of Conferences 105

SECTION 5   *Curriculum Planning* 106

5–1   Areas to Consider When Planning Curriculum 108
5–2   Program Goals 109
5–3   Program Planning 110
5–4   Curriculum Development 111
5–5   Sample Director's Calendar 112
5–6   Yearly Planner 114
5–7   Monthly Calendar 116
5–8   Unit Worksheet 117
5–9   Unit Calendar 118
5–10   Daily Planning Sheet 119
5–11   Daily Schedule 120
5–12   Parent Newsletter 121

SECTION 6   *Forms for Field Trips* 122

6–1   Sample Request for Field Trip... 124
6–2   Sample Thank You for Field Trip 125
6–3   Permission for Individual Field Trip..................................... 126
6–4   Individual Class Check-Out Form 127
6–5   Class Check-Out Chart 128
6–6   Individual Child Check-Out Form 129
6–7   Child Check-Out Chart 130
6–8   Take-Along Emergency Information Form 131
6–9   Permission for Special Outside Activity 132

SECTION 7   *Forms for Daily Record Keeping* 133

Staffing Patterns

7–1   Half-Day Program 135
7–2   Full-Day Separate Classrooms 136
7–3   Full-Day Staffing by Position 137
7–4   Licensed Capacity 138

Attendance Forms

7–5   Attendance Record... 139
7–6   Daily Time Sheet... 140

7–7   Sample Absent Child Follow-Up Letter 141

Medical/Health Related

7–8   Emergency Phone Numbers 142

7–9   Emergency Drill Log... 143

7–10 Child's Preschool Record...................................... 144

7–11 Schedule of Medications 145

7–12 Individual Child's Record of Medications Given 146

7–13 Accident Log 147

7–14 Accident Report 148

7–15 Child's Immunization Record 149

SECTION 8 *Financial Forms*.. 150

Forms Related to Tuition

8–1   Provider's Contract 152

8–2   Scholarship Application 155

8–3   Tuition Statement (Paid Per Session) 156

8–4   Tuition Statement (Based on Hourly Fee) 157

8–5   Tuition Statement (Flat Monthly Fee) 158

8–6   Tuition Reminder 159

8–7   Sample Late Payment Letter 160

Budget Forms

8–8   Income Worksheet 161

8–9   Expenses Worksheet 162

8–10 Budget Projection 163

8–11 Monthly Financial Report...................................... 164

8–12 Year-End Budget Analysis 165

SECTION 9 *Advertising Samples* 167

9–1   Fund-Raising Letter 169

9–2   Publicity Flyer 170

9–3   Elements of a News Release 171

9–4   Sample News Release 172

9–5   Newspaper Ads 173

9–6   Business Card 174

9–7   T-Shirt Logo Contest 175

9–8   T-Shirt Order Form 176

9–9   Recipe Book Letter 177

9–10 Recipe Book Order Form 178

SECTION 10 *Administrative Forms* 179

10–1 Memo 181

10–2 Messages... 182

10–3 Infants' Equipment Inventory 183

10–4 Toddlers' Equipment Inventory 184

10–5   Preschool Equipment Inventory   186

10–6   School-Age Equipment Inventory   188

10–7   Equipment Order Form   190

10–8   Supplies Order Form   191

10–9   Groceries Order Form   193

10–10   Safety Equipment Maintenance Checklist   195

10–11   Requisition Form   196

10–12   Reimbursement Form   197

10–13   Lending Library Record   198

10–14   Service Request   199

10–15   Director's Report   200

10–16   Parent Evaluation of Program   201

FORMAL STRUCTURE

The forms in this chapter will help to shape and design your program by defining the structure and your policies. If you are creating an entirely new program, this chapter will help you get started.

This set of forms can be tailored to your own unique program. Outlines are included to indicate which information needs to be addressed. The examples let you see how one program could incorporate that basic information into its functioning Articles, Bylaws, and Policies.

INITIAL ORGANIZATION

1–1 Starting a New Program suggests a path to follow in starting a new program. Your most important resource person at this point will be your licensor, but these suggestions will help you think about all of the details to be worked out. Be sure to tailor your program and facility to meet the regulations governing preschools in your city and state.

1–2/3 Articles of Incorporation Outline and Sample assist you in incorporating. When starting a new program, it is often in the best interest of the staff and, if there is one, the Board of Directors to become incorporated. This legal action provides some protection from liability for the individuals involved with the operation of the program, should there be a lawsuit. The Articles of Incorporation are based upon each state's requirements for your type of organization, and must be filed with the Secretary of State. For this step it is wise to seek the aid of an attorney so that your corporation is sure to meet all of the legal requirements of your state. The example given here is from a nonprofit organization; the structure of your Articles will be much different if yours is a private business rather than a nonprofit one.

1–4/5 Bylaws Outline and Samples are not as formal as the Articles of Incorporation, and should be much more specific in defining your program. While the Articles are kept brief and general, the Bylaws are more detailed. Again, the example is from a nonprofit organization with a Board of Directors. Bylaws need to be filed at the legal office of your preschool, but they do not need to be filed with the Secretary of State as the Articles do.

POLICIES

The Policies state specifically how your program operates from day to day. These documents are for your preschool's use only, and are therefore not filed with state records. They can be updated as needed by action of the governing board without having to go through state records. The primary justification for having well-defined policies is that decisions will be made based upon guidelines specified in writing in years to come, with new staff, new administrators, and new boards.

1–6/7 Personnel Policies Outline and Sample define the way you select, retain, and release your staff, your expectations for staff performance, and what staff members can expect in return. Personnel policies should be as specific as possible so that you have written documentation for why personnel decisions are made the way they are. Each new employee should be given a copy of the personnel policies at the time of employment.

1–8/9 Program Policies Outline and Sample define your preschool as parents see it. They include specific information about who will be admitted, when the program is in operation, and expectations of parents, children, and preschool staff. These policies are the basis for the Parent Information Booklet, Form 3–6.

1–10/11 Safety and Health Policies Outline and Sample meet the requirements of licensing agencies for written policies to ensure the health and safety of the children. These policies include procedures to follow for safety, illness, accident, natural disaster, and child abuse. They must be written carefully, reviewed regularly, and followed precisely.

Color Coding. It is helpful to color-code forms, beginning with the policies; for instance, put the personnel policies into a booklet with a red cover, and make personnel forms shades of red and pink. Student policies can have a yellow cover, and registration forms can be shades of yellow and gold. Safety and health policies and forms may be shades of blue.

STARTING A NEW PROGRAM

I. Determine a need through needs assessment, community interviews, surveys.

II. Formulate a program—population served, location, type of program, philosophy, basic functioning.

III. Plan a budget.

IV. Contact the licensing agency, i.e. public assistance, social services, human services.
   A. Notification of intent
   B. Obtain copy of regulations

V. Form a governing body/organization.
   A. Proprietorship, partnership, or board of directors
   B. Incorporation and bylaws
   C. Sponsoring agency

VI. File for tax exemption if nonprofit.

VII. Obtain start-up funding—foundations, grants, bank loans, contributions, fund-raisers.

VIII. Continue forming a program.
   A. Finalize philosophy
   B. Detail type of program
   C. Plan overall curriculum
   D. Project numbers to be served
   E. Apply for Department of Agriculture food program
   F. Plan necessary staff
   G. Plan type and size of facility
   H. Project an opening date

IX. Find a building (with money in hand!).
   A. Local zoning requirements
   B. Local and state fire regulations
   C. Remodeling—city planning commission
   D. Local and state health and sanitation requirements
   E. Check square footage, bathrooms, outdoor space against regulations
   F. Contact licensing agency again to confirm compliance

X. Purchase insurance—liability, health, accident, fire and theft, professional, corporal punishment.

XI. Check regulations for furnishings and equipment requirements; plan those purchases.

XII. Contact the post office and utilities, such as city sanitation department, gas company, electric company, and phone company.

XIII. Finalize policies and procedures, curriculum, food program plans, registration materials.

XIV. Begin advertising and taking registrations.

XV. Hire staff.

XVI. Purchase all necessary furnishings, equipment, and supplies.

XVII. Arrange a final consultation with the licensing agency; should have a license by now.

XVIII. Sponsor an event for grand opening, including thorough media coverage.

ARTICLES OF INCORPORATION
OUTLINE
Nonprofit Corporation

ARTICLE I: NAME OF CORPORATION

ARTICLE II: PURPOSE OF CORPORATION

ARTICLE III: NONPROFIT

ARTICLE IV: DURATION OF CORPORATE EXISTENCE

ARTICLE V: REGISTERED OFFICE

ARTICLE VI: INCORPORATORS

ARTICLE VII: FIRST DIRECTORS

ARTICLE VIII: PERSONAL LIABILITY

ARTICLE IX: CAPITAL STOCK

SAMPLE
ARTICLES OF INCORPORATION
Nonprofit Corporation

ARTICLE I: NAME OF CORPORATION

The name of this corporation shall be HILLSIDE PRESCHOOL.

ARTICLE II: PURPOSE OF CORPORATION

HILLSIDE PRESCHOOL is organized as a nonprofit corporation to promote, operate, and conduct a preschool for children aged three to six.

ARTICLE III: NONPROFIT

All funds collected shall be used for the above-stated purpose, and in no event shall there be any pecuniary gain to the individual members, directors, or incorporators, incidentally or otherwise.

ARTICLE IV: DURATION OF CORPORATE EXISTENCE

The period of duration of corporate existence of this corporation shall be perpetual.

ARTICLE V: REGISTERED OFFICE

The registered office of this corporation is located at:
123 Elm Street, Heartland County, Anywhere, USA 12345

ARTICLE VI: INCORPORATORS

The names and addresses of the incorporators are:

Name _____   Address _____

_____   _____

_____   _____

_____   _____

ARTICLE VII: FIRST DIRECTORS

The names, addresses, and terms of office of the first directors are:

Name _____ Address _____ Term _____

_____ _____ _____

_____ _____ _____

_____ _____ _____

FORM 1-3

ARTICLE VIII: PERSONAL LIABILITY

There shall be no personal liability for corporate obligations by any of the members, directors, or incorporators.

ARTICLE IX: CAPITAL STOCK

The corporation shall not have capital stock.

Incorporators' Signatures _____

_____

_____

_____

The foregoing instrument was acknowledged before me this _____

day of _____ , in the year _____ .

_____
Notary Public Signature

(Notarial Seal)

BYLAWS OUTLINE

ARTICLE I: NAME OF ORGANIZATION

ARTICLE II: PURPOSE OF ORGANIZATION

ARTICLE III: MEMBERSHIP

  Section A: Definition of Member

  Section B: Annual Meeting of Membership

  Section C: Place of Meetings

  Section D: Special Meetings

  Section E: Notice of Meetings

  Section F: Waiver of Notice

  Section G: Quorum

  Section H: Adjournment

  Section I: Voting

ARTICLE IV: BOARD OF DIRECTORS

  Section A: General Duties of Board of Directors

  Section B: Number, Tenure, and Qualifications

  Section C: Vacancies

  Section D: Annual Meeting

  Section E: Regular Meetings

  Section F: Special Meetings

  Section G: Notice of Meetings

  Section H: Quorum

  Section I: Voting

  Section J: Action Without a Meeting

ARTICLE V: OFFICERS

    Section A: Number

    Section B: Election and Term of Office

    Section C: Vacancies

    Section D: President

    Section E: Vice President

    Section F: Secretary

    Section G: Treasurer

    Section H: Historian

    Section I: Ex Officio Members

    Section J: Salaries

ARTICLE VI: COMMITTEES

ARTICLE VII: FISCAL YEAR

ARTICLE VIII: WAIVER

ARTICLE IX: AMENDMENTS

ARTICLE I: NAME OF ORGANIZATION

The name of this organization shall be HILLSIDE PRESCHOOL.

ARTICLE II: PURPOSE OF ORGANIZATION

HILLSIDE PRESCHOOL is organized as a nonprofit corporation to promote, operate, and conduct a preschool for children aged three to five. All funds collected shall be used for the above-stated purpose, and in no event shall there be any profit to the individual members or Directors. This corporation shall have its Registered Office at the location of the school in Anywhere, USA.

ARTICLE III: MEMBERSHIP

Section A: Definition of Member

The annual membership of the corporation consists of the parents who have children registered for the current school year and the current members of the Board of Directors. Registration shall occur when all requirements determined by the Board of Directors have been completed.

Section B: Annual Meeting of Membership

The annual meeting of the membership of the corporation shall be held on or before September 15 of each year. The purpose of the meeting shall be to elect officers of the corporation who shall serve on the Board of Directors, and for the transaction of any other business as may come before the meeting. If, for any reason, the annual meeting is not held, or the officers are not elected thereat, officers may be elected at a special meeting called for that purpose. It shall be the duty of the President, Vice President, or Secretary, upon demand of ten percent (10%) of the membership of the corporation, to call such special meeting. Should none of said officers call such meeting upon demand, the members shall have the right to call such meeting.

Section C: Place of Meetings

Meetings of the membership of the corporation shall be held at the location of the preschool unless otherwise designated by the Board of Directors.

Section D: Special Meetings

Special meetings of the membership may be called for any purpose, at any time, by the President, by the Board of Directors or a majority thereof, by the President upon written request of ten percent (10%) of the members of the corporation, or as otherwise provided in Article III, Section B hereof.

Section E: Notice of Meetings

Notice of each meeting of the membership of the corporation stating the time and place and, in the case of special meetings, the purpose, shall be given each member of the corporation not fewer than five (5) days in advance of such meetings. Giving notice shall be the responsibility of the Secretary, but proper notice by any other officer or director shall be valid.

Section F: Waiver of Notice

Notice of any meeting may be waived by any member.

Section G: Quorum

The presence of ten percent (10%) of the members of the corporation shall constitute a quorum for the transaction of business. In the absence of a quorum, no business may be transacted. Once a quorum is present, the members of the corporation may continue to transact business until adjournment, notwithstanding the withdrawal of enough members of the corporation to leave less than a quorum.

Section H: Adjournment

If any meeting of the membership of the corporation be adjourned to another time and place, no notice as to such adjourned meeting need be given provided such adjournment is approved by a majority of those entitled to vote at such meeting.

Section I: Voting

Only current members of the Board of Directors and members of the corporation in good standing may vote at any meeting of the membership of the corporation. Each member has one vote, giving a maximum of two (2) votes for each family having a child or children registered in the preschool. There shall be no absentee votes.

ARTICLE IV: BOARD OF DIRECTORS

Section A: General Duties of Board of Directors

The business and affairs of this corporation shall be governed and managed by the Board of Directors.

Section B: Number, Tenure, and Qualifications

The number of directors of the corporation shall be not fewer than five (5) nor more than nine (9) and shall include the officers of the corporation, the Director of the preschool, and the President from the preceding year, known as the Past President. Each Board member shall hold office from September 16 until September 15 of the following year. Board members must be duly qualified members of the corporation at the time they are elected, may be elected to succeed themselves in office, and shall serve without compensation. The Board of Directors shall have authority to appoint ex officio members, including, but not limited to, the teachers. Ex officio members shall not be entitled to vote at any meeting of the Board of Directors.

Section C: Vacancies

Vacancies on the Board shall not be filled unless such vacancy would bring the number of directors below the required minimum of five (5). If that would be the case, the vacancy shall be filled by appointment of any current member of the corporation by the remaining Board members.

Section D: Annual Meeting

The Board of Directors shall hold their annual meeting within one (1) week (7 days) of the annual membership meeting at which they were elected, at a time and place mutually agreed upon by a majority of the Board members.

Section E: Regular Meetings

The Board of Directors shall meet at least quarterly. The time and place for holding of regular meetings may be determined by resolution without further notice, provided that notice of such resolution is given to all Board members.

Section F: Special Meetings

Special meetings of the Board of Directors may be called for any purpose(s) at any time by the President, Vice President, or any two (2) Board members.

Section G: Notice of Meetings

Notice of any meeting shall be given at least five (5) days in advance of said meeting. Any Board member may waive notice of any meeting prior to the time of notice of such meeting. The attendance of a Board member at a meeting shall constitute a waiver of notice of such meeting.

Section H: Quorum

A simple majority of the Board of Directors shall be necessary to constitute a quorum for the transaction of business. The acts of a majority of the Board members shall be the acts of the Board of Directors.

Section I: Voting

Each Board member is entitled to one (1) vote. Absentee votes and proxies may be accepted.

Section J: Action Without a Meeting

Any action that may be taken by the Board of Directors at a meeting may be taken without a meeting if consent of all Board members shall be given.

ARTICLE V: OFFICERS

Section A: Number

The officers of the corporation shall be a President, a Vice President, a Secretary, a Treasurer, and a Historian, each of whom shall be elected to a term of office by the membership of the corporation at the annual meeting of the corporation.

Section B: Election and Term of Office

The officers shall be elected annually by the membership at the annual meeting of the corporation held on or before September 15 of each year. If the election of officers shall not be held at such time, it shall be held as soon thereafter as convenient. Each officer shall hold office until a successor is duly elected.

Section C: Vacancies

Vacancies, except in the office of President or Past President, may be filled by appointment by the remaining Board members on a temporary basis until such time as election by the membership of the corporation to fill the vacated office can be held. A vacancy in the office of President shall be filled by the duly elected Vice President. A vacancy in the office of Past President need not be filled.

Section D: President

The President shall serve a one-year term in the office of President and an additional one-year term in the capacity of Past President. The President shall be the principal executive officer of the corporation, but shall be subject to the control of the Board of Directors at all times. The President shall be responsible for carrying out the directions of the Board of Directors and, in general, supervise and control all the business and affairs of the corporation. When present, the President shall preside at all meetings of the membership of the corporation and of the Board of Directors. The President may sign, with the Secretary, all contracts or instruments which the Board of Directors has authorized to be executed.

Section E: Vice President

The Vice President shall serve a one-year term in the office of Vice President and shall automatically succeed to the office of President in the following year. The Vice President shall perform such duties as may be assigned by the Board of Directors or delegated by the President. In the absence of the President, the Vice President shall perform the duties of and have the powers of the President.

Section F: Secretary

The Secretary shall serve a two-year term, shall be elected in even-numbered years, and shall: (a) keep the minutes of the corporation meetings and the Board meetings, and file all past minutes books at the preschool office; (b) give all notices in accordance with the provisions of these bylaws; (c) be custodian of the corporate records; (d) keep a record of each member of the corporation including mailing address; (e) have power to execute any and all corporate documents along with the President; (f) file copies of all correspondence and documents relating to the preschool; and, (g) in general, perform all duties incidental to the office of Secretary and such other duties as from time to time may be assigned by the President or by the Board of Directors.

Section G: Treasurer

The Treasurer shall serve a two-year term, shall be elected in odd-numbered years, and shall: (a) have charge and custody of and be responsible for all funds of the corporation and keep all past receipts and ledgers on file at the preschool office; (b) receive and give receipts for monies due and payable or donated to the corporation from any source whatsoever, and deposit all such monies in the name of the corporation in such banks or other depositories as shall be designated by the Board of Directors; (c) keep regular books of account; and, (d) in general, perform all the duties incidental to the office of Treasurer and such other duties as from time to time may be assigned by the President or by the Board of Directors.

Section H: Historian

The Historian shall serve a one-year term. The duty shall be to record the year at preschool by collecting newspaper clippings and programs, and taking photographs of activities. These mementos are to be placed in an album and kept at the preschool to be displayed at parties and registration.

Section I: Ex Officio Members

The Ex Officio Members shall serve a one-year term and shall perform such duties as may be assigned by the President or by the Board of Directors.

Section J: Salaries

All officers shall serve without compensation.

ARTICLE VI: COMMITTEES

The Board of Directors shall have authority to establish and select chairpersons for temporary committees as they, from time to time, deem advisable. Any permanent committee(s) must be created by a vote of the membership of the corporation to amend these bylaws accordingly.

ARTICLE VII: FISCAL YEAR

The fiscal year of this corporation shall begin on the first day of September and end on the 31st day of August of the following year.

ARTICLE VIII: WAIVER

Whenever any notice is required under the provisions of these Bylaws, the Articles of Incorporation, or under provisions of the State Nonprofit Corporation Act, a signed waiver thereof in writing, whether before or after the time, shall be deemed equivalent to the giving of such notice.

ARTICLE IX: AMENDMENTS

The Articles of Incorporation or the Bylaws of this corporation may be amended as provided by the corporation laws of the State.

Adopted by the membership of HILLSIDE PRESCHOOL, Incorporated this _____ day of _____ , in the year _____ .

Signed: _____
President

Signed: _____
Secretary

I. HIRING

II. STAFF EVALUATION

III. JOB DESCRIPTIONS

IV. PROMOTIONS AND SALARY INCREMENTS

V. FIRING

VI. BENEFITS

VII. WORKING HOURS

VIII. SUBSTITUTE STAFF ARRANGEMENTS

IX. HEALTH REQUIREMENTS

X. IN-SERVICE AND SEMINARS

XI. CONFIDENTIALITY

XII. TUITION OF STAFF CHILDREN

I. HIRING

A. In employment of staff, the preschool advertises openings through the public media to make the position known to all, and does not discriminate on the basis of race, creed, color, national origin, religion, sex, or on the basis of physical and/or mental handicap when the handicap would not prevent fulfillment of normal job responsibilities.

B. When a vacancy occurs in the staff, the method of choice to fill the position is to promote a current employee. Consideration is given to employees based on their education and experience, their length of employment in this program, total in-service and extra courses since joining the staff, and the sum of the annual evaluations.

C. Minimum requirements for all staff positions are: 18 years old, good moral character, and a genuine interest in and love for young children. Experience with children is preferred.
   1. Any staff member who has been convicted of a felony or has been involved with a child abuse or neglect court action or official investigation shall be required to provide information relative to the conviction and evidence of suitability for his/her position in the preschool.
   2. Minimum educational requirement for a teacher is a four-year degree, preferably in education or a closely related field.
   3. Minimum requirement for a director is at least a four-year degree in education or a closely related field, and experience in an early childhood program.

D. A resume is required of each applicant for a teacher's or director's position. Resumes are accepted, then an *Application for Employment* is completed by each of the most qualified applicants.

E. Final applicants must submit three *Reference Information* forms, and are then interviewed by the Director and/or Board of Directors.

F. The Director shall have the three *Reference Information* forms on file with the licensing agency attesting to his/her character and child caring ability. The references shall include persons who have personal knowledge of his/her ability to care for children.

G. It is the responsibility of the Director to attest to the good moral character of all employees and other persons who come in contact with the children. This will be done by collecting three *Reference Information* forms for each employee and volunteer. These shall remain on file for review.

H. The hiring of teachers, aides, and support staff shall be the duty of the Director, with the approval of the Board. The hiring of a Director shall be a Board decision.

I. Each newly hired staff member shall be given a packet consisting of:
   1. *Job Description*
   2. *Bylaws*
   3. Policies
   4. *Reference Information* forms to be completed and returned
   5. *Medical Report* form to be completed and returned
   6. New Student Registration Packet

J. The Board shall complete a *Contract for Employment* specifying terms of employment, to be signed by the staff member and the Board President and Secretary.

K. Each new staff member is hired conditionally for a probation period of three months while performing the regular duties of the position.

II. STAFF EVALUATION

A. Staff evaluation shall be conducted at the end of the three-month probationary period and at the end of each school year. It shall be a composite of:
   1. *Parent Evaluation of Program* sent home in one of the final newsletters of the year
   2. *Staff Evaluation* completed by the Director and/or Board
   3. Teacher self-evaluation

B. Evaluation shall cover the following areas:
   1. Fulfillment of job obligations as stated in *Job Description* and *Contract for Employment*
   2. Compliance with state standards
   3. Compliance with objectives and goals of the program as stated in the Policies and as administered by the Director
   4. Physical, mental, and emotional competence to care for children
   5. Dependability and reliability
   6. Initiative in implementing the program
   7. Willingness to share the workload
   8. Relationship with other staff, Board, parents, and children
   9. Attendance, promptness
   10. Appropriate appearance

III. JOB DESCRIPTIONS

A. See attached forms for:
   1. Director
   2. Teacher
   3. Teacher's Aide
   4. Substitute Teacher
   5. Cook
   6. Bus Driver
   7. Maintenance/Housekeeping
   8. Secretary
   9. Bookkeeper

B. During the year the Board will require all staff to participate in the following events:
   1. Fall registration
   2. End-of-year clean-up sessions
   3. Regular staff meetings

C. In addition to the above, teaching staff will be required to participate in the following events each year:
   1. Fall and spring parent-teacher conferences
   2. Spring preregistration open house
   3. At least one continuing education seminar/workshop
   4. A choice of at least one of the following:
      a. Celebration of the Week of the Young Child
      b. End-of-year, all-school skating party
      c. Fund raiser to be decided upon by the Board

IV. PROMOTIONS AND SALARY INCREMENTS

A. A promotion is an increase in responsibility with corresponding increase in salary.

B. Promotions will be granted only if positions are available and qualifications are met.

C. Any staff member earning a CDA or academic credential while employed will be given an immediate raise and, when possible, a promotion.

D. Raises are attempted annually, but depend upon the current and projected financial status of the preschool.

E. A raise is figured as a percentage of the staff member's current salary.

V. FIRING

A. The Director and/or Board members must document staff incompetencies in the areas listed above under Item II. Staff Evaluation.

B. Justification for firing is violation of any of the above.

C. The staff member will have the right to defend him/herself before the Board.

D. The decision to fire must be by a majority of the Board.

VI. BENEFITS

A. Paid personal, sick, and vacation leave are earned as specified in the *Contract for Employment,* and may be taken at the staff member's discretion.

B. Holidays listed on the accompanying *Calendar of Holidays* are paid holidays.

C. Social security and worker's compensation are paid by the preschool.

D. Insurance is available for employees to purchase through a group plan.

VII. WORKING HOURS

A. The program is in session from the Tuesday after Labor Day through the Friday before Memorial Day, Monday through Friday, with the exception of the holidays listed on the attached *Calendar of Holidays.*

B. Working hours vary, and are detailed in the employee's contract.

VIII. SUBSTITUTE STAFF ARRANGEMENTS

A. The Director may arrange for substitutes, or the staff may arrange for the substitute with the Director's approval.

B. Hours are the same as the staff member being substituted for.

C. Substitute staff is paid on an hourly basis, the rate to be determined at the time of employment.

IX. HEALTH REQUIREMENTS

A. Record of a TB test within the last five years.

B. A completed *Medical Report Form,* which is obtained from the licensing agency.

C. A staff member with a communicable disease must take leave until no longer contagious.

X. IN-SERVICE AND SEMINARS

A. Staff members are expected to attend at least one training or in-service session per year. Additional training is encouraged.

B. The preschool will pay registration fees.

C. The preschool will pay additional fees such as mileage, room, and/or board as funds will allow.

D. Taking time off in order to attend training sessions during work hours will be considered the same as working time, and it will be paid as such.

XI. CONFIDENTIALITY

A. Student's records are open only to the particular student's teacher, the Director, an authorized employee of the licensing agency, or the child's parent or legal guardian.

B. Staff personnel records are open only to that staff member, the Director, an authorized employee of the licensing agency, or the Board of Directors.

XII. TUITION OF STAFF CHILDREN

Full tuition plus the equipment fee are to be paid by children of staff and Board members.

PROGRAM POLICIES OUTLINE

I. AFFIRMATIVE ACTION STATEMENT

II. ADMISSIONS

III. CALENDAR YEAR

IV. DAYS AND HOURS OF OPERATION

V. PICK-UP AND DELIVERY OF STUDENTS

VI. PROGRAM

VII. FEES

VIII. CONFIDENTIALITY OF STUDENT RECORDS

IX. DISCIPLINE

X. COMMUNICATIONS WITH PARENTS

XI. DRESS

XII. FOODS

FORM 1-8

SAMPLE
PROGRAM POLICIES

I. AFFIRMATIVE ACTION STATEMENT

The preschool advertises for children in the public media in order to make openings known to all. Children are admitted regardless of race, creed, color, sex, national origin, religion, or handicapping condition.

II. ADMISSIONS

Children who are 3 years old up to kindergarten age are eligible to enroll in the preschool. Admission requirements and enrollment procedures are as follows:

A. A child must be 3 years old by September 1 to be admitted into the 3-year-old class.

B. Children in the 3-year-old class will not be allowed to advance into the 4-year-old class during the school year.

C. A child must be 4 years old by September 1 to be admitted into the 4-year-old class.

D. If a parent intends to enroll a child in kindergarten before the standard age of 5, and if the parent can provide written verification by the school system that the child will be attending kindergarten the following school year, then the child may be enrolled in the 4-year-old class.

E. The Director will meet with the parents or guardians of a child with special needs at the time of enrollment. A planning session will be held with the child's parents or guardians, health and/or education specialists, and the Director and classroom staff to plan an *Individualized Plan for Child with Special Needs.* The same committee will meet quarterly to reevaluate the child's progress.

F. Classes are filled on a first-come/first-served basis according to the date of enrollment with the Director.

G. If the classes are filled when a parent calls, the child's name will be put on a waiting list to fill vacancies as they occur.

H. Parents of enrolled children receive a letter in the fall inviting them to the registration meeting, where registration is completed.

I. As vacancies occur during the year, they will be filled from the waiting list, or from new registrations according to the above procedures.

III. CALENDAR YEAR

The calendar year is from the Tuesday after Labor Day to the Friday before Memorial Day. The preschool observes the holidays listed on the attached *Calendar of Holidays.*

IV. DAYS AND HOURS OF OPERATION

The preschool is in session from 8:00 A.M. to 5:00 P.M., Monday through Friday.

V. PICK-UP AND DELIVERY OF CHILDREN

No child is to be brought before 8:00 A.M., nor picked up after 5:00 P.M. If a child is left beyond 5:00 P.M. with no arrangements made, a babysitting fee will be assessed when the child is picked up.

For safety's sake, children must never be left without direct transfer to an adult; therefore children must always be brought directly to the classroom. Parents must return to the classroom to pick up their children.

VI. PROGRAM

It is the philosophy of this preschool that early childhood should be a time of fun, warmth, security, exploring, and discovery. Preschool children are creative and receptive; the program strives to nurture and encourage these qualities in its students.

The preschool's purpose is to provide an atmosphere that encourages social, emotional, physical, and intellectual growth and development of the child as a whole.

Planned within the framework of philosophy and purpose, the curriculum includes sharing and conversation time; stories, songs, and fingerplays; creative art activities and crafts; games and large muscle activities; field trips throughout the community; food preparation; science and nature activities; exposure to shapes, colors, numbers, and letters; and celebration of birthdays and holidays.

VII. FEES

Tuition is figured as a monthly fee. It is to be paid in advance each month, by the 5th of the month. Because tuition is a monthly fee, no refunds are given for illness, vacations, or snow days unless the absence is for more than five consecutive school days. In such a case, a refund must be considered individually with the Director.

At registration the first tuition payment is due, as well as the annual equipment fee, which is paid by each student regardless of arrangements made for payment of tuition.

In the event that tuition payments are late, parents will be given up to one month to make restitution. If after one month, payment has not been made, the child will be refused admission to the preschool, and further action will be taken against the parents.

Either full or partial payment will be accepted from a human services organization. Application forms and a contract must be completed at the time of enrollment.

If the parents are unable to pay tuition due to economic conditions, they may apply to the Board for consideration for the scholarship fund. The Board will consider applications for scholarship funds on a case-by-case basis.

VIII. CONFIDENTIALITY OF STUDENT RECORDS

Student records are open only to the particular child's teacher, the Director, an authorized employee of the licensing agency, or the child's parent or legal guardian.

IX. DISCIPLINE

Acceptable behavior is encouraged by giving positive verbal rewards. This reinforces a child's good feeling about his/her behavior and serves as an example to the other children to act in such a way as to receive this praise. Asking a child to stop and think about his/her unpleasant behavior enables that child to work at self-control.

For a child not cooperating in a group listening situation, the child is seated by a teacher and reminded of acceptable behavior.

Removal from the group for a period of "time-out" is the next tactic used for a child who continually demonstrates unacceptable behavior. This time-out is not a punishment, but rather a time when the child may calm down, remember what behavior the teacher is asking for, and decide for him- or herself when he/she is ready to rejoin the group with appropriate behavior.

Corporal punishment is not an accepted method of dealing with young children's behavior. Children will not be hit, slapped, or spanked in any manner while attending this preschool.

If behavior problems persist, the parents are asked to a conference to discuss what may be helpful in motivating their child to behave in an acceptable way. It may be suggested that the child be involved in a behavior modification program, with the parents having the option of being involved in the process.

X. COMMUNICATIONS WITH PARENTS

Parents are informed of the activities of the preschool through weekly newsletters. The *Parent Newsletter* will include weekly unit topics, class activities, field trips, and suggestions for parents.

There will be two parent conferences offered during the year, one in the fall and one in the spring. Either the parents or teachers may request an additional conference any time there is a special concern.

Parents are encouraged to visit the preschool at any time. Because of occasional field trips and special activities, advance notice is suggested.

XI. DRESS

Children are encouraged to wear play clothes and tennis shoes. Daily activities include active and messy play, and the children should feel comfortable enough to enjoy themselves without worrying about their clothes. The child's name should be placed in all outdoor clothing and other belongings to help ensure the return of all the proper possessions and clothes.

Special preschool logo t-shirts are available for parents to purchase for their child. The staff encourages the children to wear their t-shirts on all field trips and outings.

XII. FOODS

Children should have eaten breakfast before they arrive in the morning. Snacks are furnished mid-morning and mid-afternoon. Snacks are used as a part of the curriculum, often related to the unit topic, and as an experience in tasting. A nutritionally balanced lunch is served each day; lunch menus are posted for a month in advance.

With advance notice, children may bring special treats for their birthday or any other time during the year. Because of state regulations regarding the serving of food, the treats must be purchased commercially, either prepackaged or from a bakery.

SAFETY AND HEALTH POLICIES OUTLINE

I. SAFETY POLICIES

A. Prevention

B. Emergencies

1. Fire
2. Tornado
3. Earthquake
4. Blizzard
5. Power Failure
6. Missing Person
7. Transportation

II. HEALTH POLICIES

A. Staff Health

B. Children's Health

1. Health Care Summary
2. Exclusion of Sick Child
3. Emergency Authorization
4. Emergency Procedures
5. Medications
6. Sick Room
7. General Cleanliness

III. CHILD ABUSE

I. SAFETY POLICIES

The staff is informed of safety rules, special hazards, and commonly occurring accidents. They receive detailed instruction on evacuation procedures, use of fire extinguishers, and how to report an accident. There is one staff member on duty at all times who has a current first aid certificate.

The Health Consultant or Director conducts such staff training and also inspects the facility for hazards twice each year.

A. Prevention

The children are under direct adult supervision at all times. Fighting is not allowed; running and throwing of objects are not allowed except as a supervised part of the curriculum.

All poisonous substances are stored in a locked cupboard out of the reach of children. Medications are not stored in the same cupboard as poisonous materials.

No toys or equipment with easily removable small parts (eyes, wheels, etc.) are allowed. No suckers or hard candies are allowed.

All sharp objects are stored out of reach of the children. Such objects as scissors are used only under direct supervision. The classroom equipment is observed continually for stability, smoothness of wooden objects, and safe corners.

All shelving is securely fastened to the walls. The water heater and other gas appliances are bolted down to the floor.

The play yard is fenced, and no child is allowed outside to play unless there is a staff member present.

All electric outlets are capped. The furnace room door is locked, and that room is off limits except to staff. Flammable materials are stored in a separate cupboard (may be with poisons) out of the children's reach. This cupboard is not near any flame or heat source, nor is it near an exit to the building or doorways to other rooms. The hot water temperature does not exceed 120 degrees. Electrical appliances are used by staff members only. Whenever cooking is done as a part of the curriculum, the children are cautioned and under the direct supervision of staff. Electrical appliances and matches are stored out of reach when not in use. Any hot surfaces—pipes, radiators, etc.—are protected by guards.

The locations of the fuse box, the main electrical power switch, and the gas and water main valves are known to each staff member. The electricity shall be cut off at the main switch in the event of electrical fire, earthquake, or tornado warning. Following an earthquake, gas, electrical, and water lines are checked carefully for breaks or leaks.

Stairways are kept clear at all times. Handrailings are available at the proper height and are kept in good repair.

At any time the children leave the building as a group, they are required to walk in an orderly fashion and are accompanied by the staff, and other adults if deemed necessary. Parents are required to bring their children into the building, and pick them up inside each day. No child is to go out to a car alone.

B. Emergencies

1. Fire

The preschool conforms to all fire regulations as designated by the State Fire Marshall. A fire evacuation plan and alternate is drawn and posted in the school.

The 911 emergency number and the exact address of the building are posted by the telephone.

Monthly fire drills are held. The fire alarm system, emergency power pack lights, and fire extinguishers are checked yearly for proper function. All staff members know how to use the fire extinguishers.

In the event of a fire, the building shall be immediately evacuated. The staff member in charge shall phone the fire department from within the building, if it is safe, or from another phone. A designated staff member may attempt to extinguish the fire while the building is being evacuated. All other staff members are to remain with the children and see them safely to the designated emergency shelter.

2. Tornado

A written tornado shelter plan is posted. Tornado drills are held monthly from April through September.

A battery-operated radio is easily accessible and kept in good repair. In case of an emergency, staff will tune to the local radio station for tornado information.

In the event of a tornado warning, the children shall be evacuated to the designated area—a basement if one is available, a nearby building or under furniture within the building—and remain there until the threat has passed.

3. Earthquake

A written earthquake plan is posted. Earthquake drills are held monthly.

A battery-operated radio is easily accessible and kept in good repair. In case of an emergency, staff will tune to the local radio station for earthquake information.

In the event of an earthquake, if the children are indoors they will be kept indoors and seated on the floor along the inside walls. If the children are outside, they will be kept outside in the open, away from buildings and utility wires. After the quake, the children will be kept together where they are until one staff member can inspect the premises for damage.

4. Blizzard

In the event of a blizzard when parents are not able to pick up their children, the staff will house the children at the facility until the parents or guardians can pick them up. Arrangements have been made with a local grocery store for the delivery of food should such an emergency arise.

5. Power Failure

Two flashlights in working order are kept in an accessible place. Power pack emergency lights are installed to light each exit.

6. Missing Person

Should a child be missing, staff shall search the building and grounds completely. If the child is still not found, the police and parent/guardian shall be notified while staff begin searching the immediate surrounding area.

7. Transportation

While transporting children on a field trip, each child is securely buckled into a child safety device appropriate to his/her age and weight.

If there is more than one vehicle, the drivers stay together as much as possible and watch out for each other. If a vehicle should break down, all the vehicles shall stop. One adult shall go telephone for help while the others remain with the children. The Director shall be called to arrange alternative tansportation. All adults shall then remain with the children until such transportation arrives.

II. HEALTH POLICIES

The Director is responsible for observing the health and development of children, handling illness, implementing accident prevention and emergency procedures, keeping health records complete and current, and informing parents of community resources. Some or all of these duties may be shared with, or delegated to, other staff members.

Continuing health consultation is sought from a physician, PHN, or RN with training in dealing with children. The consultant assists in developing health policies and keeping them current, assists in screening referral and follow-up procedures, and provides advice about children with special needs. The consultant reviews health policies, health records, any health problems, and the *Accident Log* with the Director twice a year. The consultant also checks the first aid kit, the sick room area, and safety conditions. The twice-yearly inspection and any recommendations for change are noted in writing. Any necessary changes are made to conform to health and safety standards within 30 days of notice of inspection.

A. Staff Health

Prior to employment, each employee must submit a *Medical Report Form* signed by his/her source of medical care based on a thorough examination within three months. Statements must be submitted every two years thereafter.

All staff must submit evidence of freedom from tuberculosis before employment. If a mantoux test proves negative, no further evidence is necessary; if the mantoux is positive, a chest x-ray must be taken. If the x-ray is negative, such evidence is sufficient, but the x-ray must be repeated every two years. A positive x-ray prevents employment.

Any employee who contracts a communicable disease that presents a health hazard to the children is put on immediate sick leave. Following a serious illness, a signed statement from the employee's doctor stating freedom from infection is required to return to work.

B. Children's Health

1. Health Care Summary
Each child is required to have on file a health statement, obtained from the licensing agency, which includes a record of up-to-date immunizations and the signature of the child's source of medical care. If a child's health care summary is not complete at the time of enrollment or within 30 days after enrollment, the child will be excluded from the program.

Each child who has not had a physical examination within the last year must have one before entrance into the program. This physical may be done by a physician, public health nurse, or preschool screening clinic.

2. Exclusion of Sick Child
No child who arrives noticeably ill, with a rash, or with a fever shall be admitted for that day. Should a child become ill during the day, he/she will go to the sick room and remain there under adult supervision until a parent or authorized person arrives to take the child home.

In the event a child contracts a communicable disease and exposes the other children, notice of such exposure will be posted, and parents will be notified when they pick up their children. The sick child will not be allowed to return to school until the period of contagion has passed.

3. Emergency Authorization
The preschool must have on file for each child a signed *Permission for Health Care* authorizing emergency care and transfer of medical records to the local hospital. Emergency numbers for reaching the parent or guardian and another authorized person shall also be on file.

4. Emergency Procedures
At least one staff member on duty at all times has first aid training through an accredited course. All other staff members are trained in emergency procedures through annual in-service.

The child's parent, guardian, or authorized person shall be notified immediately in the event of a serious accident or illness requiring emergency care. First aid shall be administered by a qualified staff member.

The 911 emergency number is posted by the telephone. The local rescue squad or ambulance service shall provide emergency transportation; the local hospital shall provide emergency care.

In the event that a child is transported to the hospital, his/her health summary and signed *Permission for Health Care* shall be sent along. A staff member shall accompany the child until the arrival of the parents, guardian, or authorized person.

An *Accident Report* shall be completed for each accident except minor scratches and abrasions. The report shall be made as soon as possible following the accident and no later than the same day. The original report shall be filed in the child's file, one copy shall be filed in the *Accident Log,* and one copy shall be given to the parent. The words "Accident—see teacher" shall be recorded in the comments column of the *Daily Time Sheet* behind the child's name so that the parent will be made aware of the accident, can discuss it with the staff, and be given the copy of the report.

5. Medications
Medications are kept in a locked cupboard out of reach of the children.

Any nonprescription medication to be administered at school, such as aspirin, cough syrup, or sun screen, must be accompanied by the parent's written permission and instructions for use.

Any prescription medication to be administered by a staff member must be in its original container and be labeled. The label is to contain the child's name, physician's name, pharmacist, medication, dosage, frequency, starting date, and expiration date if applicable. This information is checked when receiving the medication from the parent. An *Individual Child's Record of Medication Given* is signed by the parent/guardian authorizing its administration.

A schedule of medications is posted on the drug cabinet:

Date	Name	Medication	Dose	Times	Stop
1/5/90	Amy Smith	Penicillin	1 tsp.	8-12-4	1/15/90

A staff member shall triple check the label before administering the medication—once before opening, once after opening, and once after closing container. After the medicine has been completed, the *Individual Child's Record of Medication Given* shall be filed with the child's health record.

Any drug container having a detached, excessively soiled, or damaged label is returned to the parent for relabeling by the pharmacist. Any contents of any drug container without a label or with an illegible label are destroyed immediately.

© 1990 by The Center for Applied Research in Education, Inc.

FORM 1-11

Any unused portions of prescription drugs are returned to the parent or destroyed by the Director by flushing them into the sewer and removing and destroying the labels from the drug containers.

Medications having a specific expiration date are not used after the date of expiration.

The parent must be informed when any medication is given.

6. Sick Room

An area is isolated from the remainder of the program by a screen or wall for the purpose of health care. This area contains a cot, washable linens, blanket, and pillow for the use of any person who is ill or injured.

Also contained in this area is a locked cupboard or out-of-reach cabinet for the storage of medications, a ten-unit first aid kit, thermometer, emesis basin, wastebasket, goose neck lamp, a first aid book or instructions, and any other health care supplies.

7. General Cleanliness

Children are encouraged and helped to keep themselves clean. Paper towels are provided for their use. Children are supervised in toileting and washing hands. They receive age-appropriate training in personal hygiene to include proper hand washing methods, time to wash hands, proper toileting procedure, and proper hair care.

III. CHILD ABUSE

Should staff suspect possible child abuse or neglect, observations and dates must be documented on the *Observation of Child Problem* form. The staff member must inform the Director, who in turn must notify the local family services agency.

Any suspicion of abuse by staff at the preschool must be documented on the *Documentation of Employment Problem* form and reported immediately to the Director. The Director will confer with the staff member, then report to the local family services agency and the Board of Directors if the Director determines that abuse is a possibility.

Procedures outlined by family services must be followed. The staff member will have the opportunity for defense before the Board of Directors.

SECTION 2
PERSONNEL FORMS

The forms in this section were developed to assist in hiring new staff, delineating job responsibilities, documenting personnel action, and recording staff training. They were designed to facilitate comprehensive record-keeping by busy administrators.

APPLICATION FORMS

2–1 Application for Employment is a very general application form that can be used in combination with a resume using the first page only, or without a resume using both pages. If both the first and second pages are used, then omit the sentence reading "Please attach a resume detailing education and employment history."

2–2 Personnel Attitudes Survey is a tool to assess the feeling a prospective employee has for children. There is no method of "correction" since it is meant only to convey attitudes. It should be completed at the employment interview in about ten minutes. It is more helpful if applicants are not allowed time to ponder and perhaps invent answers that they think the interviewer wants.

2–3 Interview Rating Form is meant to be an objective method of assessing the applicant's qualifications by rating the answers given on a scale of 1 to 10. You may wish to take notes on the answers given during the interview, then go back to the form after the interview to rate the answers. It also works well to have one person doing the interviewing and another taking the notes, so that at least one person is giving full attention while the applicant speaks.

2–4/5 Reference Cover Letter and Reference Information go together to the persons an applicant has listed as references. The applicant's name fits into the first paragraph of the body of the letter, as well as on the top line of the form.

JOB DESCRIPTIONS

2–6/15 Job Descriptions are meant to be a starting point, adapting them to meet the needs of your program. The job description for the Director is written for a half-day preschool program where the Director is responsible to the Board of Directors. Likewise the **Responsibilities**

of the Board of Directors is written for the same preschool program with volunteer officers rather than paid support staff.

2–16 Parental Responsibilities is an attempt to put into clear, concise form just what is expected of parents. The intent is to make the list as short as possible, yet include each of those things on which you stand firm so that there is no misunderstanding.

EMPLOYMENT FORMS

2–17 Contract for Employment is a form that is general enough to be used for any of the positions within the teaching or support staff, although the information supplied should be very specific. Two copies of it should be signed so that the employee and the employer may each keep one on file. Note that it is intended to be used with the *Personnel Policies, Job Description,* and *Calendar of Holidays.*

2–18 Employee Time Sheet is used by each employee to record hours worked during each pay period.

2–19 Substitute Time Sheet is used by substitutes to record identifying information, for what position they are substituting, and hours worked during each pay period.

2–20 Request for Leave is used by the employee to request time off. After the top is completed by the employee, the bottom is completed by the supervisor. The form is then copied, and the copy is returned to the employee while the original is filed in the employee's personnel file.

2–21 Criteria for Self-Evaluation of Program is a condensation of the *Parent Evaluation of Program* that is completed by parents at the end of the year. These same items may be used by each staff member for self-evaluation and as a basis for self-improvement.

2–22 Staff Evaluation can be used for any teaching or support staff. It is intended to be used annually, with the employee completing one form and the supervisor completing another separately. The two should then come together to discuss the evaluation. The results from each, as well as the average of the scores from the parents' evaluations, can then be recorded onto the supervisor's evaluation; the originals of each evaluation should be filed in the personnel file, and a copy of each should be given to the employee.

2–23 Letter of Reference is the document to use when a letter of reference is requested regarding a current or former employee. The information is taken directly from the latest annual *Staff Evaluation* with space for more personal comments at the bottom.

2–24 Award for Excellence is a fun way to acknowledge the special contribution made by an employee. The employee's name goes on the first line, and the reason for the award goes on the second. It can either be posted or given to the employee.

2–25 Employee Complaint is to be completed by an employee who has a complaint about working conditions, policies, a supervisor, a co-worker, and so on. It acknowledges that the employee has a right to be heard and taken seriously.

There should be easy access to the forms and a nonthreatening way to submit them. Whether the supervisor chooses to handle the situation alone or requests a conference with the employee, the bottom of the form should be completed. The original is to be filed in the employee's personnel file, and a copy returned to the employee.

2–26 Documentation of Employment Problem is to be completed by the supervisor when there is a complaint about an employee. Any action taken against an employee is easier when there has been documentation of the problem over time.

If the matter is discussed with the employee, then a copy of the completed form may be given to the employee, either during the meeting or when making the appointment, to give the employee time to form a response.

2–27 Supervisor/Staff Conference is the documentation of a meeting between supervisor and employee to discuss an issue brought up by either of them. The intent of this form is to eliminate, insofar as possible, misunderstandings about what was said during a confrontation.

Each is given the opportunity to express his/her point of view after the conversation, and to read the point of view of the other. The employee is then given a copy of this form, while the original is filed in the personnel file.

CONTINUING EDUCATION FORMS

2–28 Certificate of Training is the documentation of attendance at a workshop or seminar for continuing education. It may be used by any staff member, for any type of training. The staff member may complete the whole form and have it signed or stamped by whomever is conducting the training.

2–29 Record of Continuing Education can be kept both by the employee for his/her own records, as well as by the employer in the staff member's personnel file. The information can be taken from the *Certificate of Training*.

2–30 Evaluation of Training is to be completed by each staff member who has attended a training session as soon as possible after the training. If appropriate, a copy of the evaluation can be sent to the presentor.

2–31 Voucher for Travel Expenses is to be used by the employee to request reimbursement for expenses incurred while representing the program or while attending training. All receipts are to be attached to document spending.

APPLICATION FOR EMPLOYMENT

Date of application _____

Position applied for _____

Name _____
        (Last)   (First)   (Middle)

Address _____

Telephone _____ Social Security number _____

On what date would you be available for work? _____

Do you have any physical, mental, or medical impairment or disability that would limit your job performance in the position for which you are applying? _____

If yes, please explain _____
_____

Have you ever been convicted of a felony, or been involved with a child abuse or neglect court action or official investigation? Yes _____ No _____

If yes, please explain _____
_____

List memberships in professional or business organizations:
_____
_____

Give the names, addresses, and telephone numbers of three references who are not related to you and who are not previous employers:
_____
_____
_____

PLEASE ATTACH A RESUME DETAILING EDUCATION AND EMPLOYMENT HISTORY.

EDUCATION

College	Location	Dates	Major	Degree

High School	Location	Dates	Program	Graduate

Special Organizations/Honors _____
_____
_____

EMPLOYMENT HISTORY (most recent first)

Position _____ Dates _____

Duties _____

Employer _____

Address _____

Supervisor _____ Phone _____

Position _____ Dates _____

Duties _____

Employer _____

Address _____

Supervisor _____ Phone _____

Position _____ Dates _____

Duties _____

Employer _____

Address _____

Supervisor _____ Phone _____

Position _____ Dates _____

Duties _____

Employer _____

Address _____

Supervisor _____ Phone _____

VOLUNTEER EXPERIENCE (most recent first)

Position _____ Dates _____

Duties _____

Organization _____

Address _____

Supervisor _____ Phone _____

Position _____ Dates _____

Duties _____

Organization _____

Address _____

Supervisor _____ Phone _____

ADDITIONAL SKILLS

_____

_____

34

PERSONNEL ATTITUDES SURVEY

These phrases refer to 2- to 6-year-old children and to teaching them in a preschool situation. Please complete each phrase in as few words as possible. Complete them quickly, briefly, and honestly. There are no right answers, only the way you feel.

1. Children are wonderful, but _____

_____

2. When a child cries, it makes me feel like _____

_____

3. When I speak to children _____

_____

4. Children who are not potty trained _____

_____

5. What children *want* to make them happy is _____

_____

6. What children *need* most is _____

_____

7. A child feels unhappy when _____

_____

8. Children are naughty because _____

_____

9. Children who "pretend" _____

_____

10. Friends are important to children because _____

_____

11. Children get into everything because _____

_____

12. Children learn the most when _____

_____

13. Children's art _____

_____

14. Before children go to kindergarten they should know _____

_____

15. My favorite activity with children is _____

_____

16. My favorite story or picture book for children is _____

_____

17. My favorite children's game is _____

_____

18. My favorite TV show for children is _____
_____

19. Something that always makes me smile is _____
_____

20. Something that makes me so angry is _____
_____

21. When I first get up in the morning, I feel _____
_____

22. My childhood was _____
_____

23. What I consider a real mess is _____
_____

24. The kind of mess that doesn't bother me is _____
_____

25. The teacher I remember most from my childhood (describe the teacher) _____
_____

26. Teachers need _____
_____

27. Teachers should _____
_____

28. Supervisors _____
_____

29. I am easy to get along with because _____
_____

30. I think my two most important jobs as a preschool teacher will be _____
_____

31. Preschool should be _____
_____

32. I want to work at this preschool because _____
_____

INTERVIEW RATING FORM

Name of Applicant _____

Date _____

Interviewers _____

_____

_____

© 1990 by The Center for Applied Research in Education, Inc.

Each answer is rated on a scale of 1–10, with 10 being "the best" and 1 being "the worst."

1. Please tell us about yourself, and in doing so touch upon your educational background, your experience, and your interests.

          10   9   8   7   6   5   4   3   2   1

2. Why did you apply for this position?

          10   9   8   7   6   5   4   3   2   1

3. What is your philosophy of preschool education?

          10   9   8   7   6   5   4   3   2   1

4. How would you handle each of these situations in your classroom?
A child hitting another child

          10   9   8   7   6   5   4   3   2   1

A child disrupting group activities and interrupting the teacher

          10   9   8   7   6   5   4   3   2   1

A child having difficulty in finishing a given task

          10   9   8   7   6   5   4   3   2   1

A withdrawn child

          10   9   8   7   6   5   4   3   2   1

5. During an activity a 3-year-old tells you that his dad hit him several times. You and a co-worker notice bruises on the child. What would you do?

          10   9   8   7   6   5   4   3   2   1

6. What are some examples of unit topics that you would like to teach to preschool-aged children?

          10   9   8   7   6   5   4   3   2   1

7. How do you see your position in relation to the rest of the staff?

          10   9   8   7   6   5   4   3   2   1

Total number of points: _____
(Maximum of 100)

REFERENCE COVER LETTER

(Your letterhead)

(Inside Address)

Dear _____ ,

_____ has furnished your name as a reference to provide information regarding his/her suitability to care for young children.

Please complete the enclosed questionnaire and return it to the above address as soon as possible. Any comments you care to make will be welcomed, and may be added on the back of the questionnaire.

Thank you for your cooperation in this matter.

Sincerely,

REFERENCE INFORMATION

Reference for _____

How long have you known this person? _____

What is the nature of your relationship with this person? _____

_____

Does this person appear to be in good health, and physically and mentally able to care for children? _____

_____

How often have you observed this person with children? _____

_____

How would you rate this person's general interest in children? _____

_____

How would you rate this person's understanding of children and their special needs? __

_____

How does this person handle the discipline of children? _____

_____

Has this person ever been suspected or convicted of child neglect or abuse? _____

_____

Would you permit this person to care for your child? _____

_____

_____

_____

_____
Signature/Date

JOB DESCRIPTION—DIRECTOR

QUALIFICATIONS

1. Have three *Reference Information Forms* on file with the licensing agency, attesting to character and child caring ability
2. Demonstrate education or training in child care and practical experience
3. Be a degreed teacher
4. Exhibit enthusiasm and energy towards the children, staff, and preschool
5. Attend continuing education seminars/workshops

LICENSING

1. Make application for and receive the license from the licensing agency annually
2. Maintain state standards in program, staff, and facility
3. Meet with fire and sanitation officials as they make their annual inspections
4. Comply with recommendations made at such inspections, and inform proper authorities of compliance in writing
5. Insure that regular emergency drills are held in each class

STAFF SUPERVISION

1. Hire personnel
2. Arrange for new employee orientation
3. Maintain staff personnel files to include resume, *Application for Employment, Medical Report,* three *Reference Information Forms,* and *Staff Evaluation Forms* for each employee
4. Maintain staff ratio, assigning staff and students to classes
5. Arrange for substitute staff
6. Meet at least monthly with staff to oversee curriculum planning, staff performance, problems, and/or commendations
7. Organize any appropriate in-service training or other extracurricular activities

REGISTRATION

1. Advertise for enrollment
2. Register students throughout the year
3. Write and mail to parents by September 1 the fall *Registration Letter,* including all necessary information and the year's *School Calendar*
4. Make arrangements for the use of the building for all activities outside of regular preschool hours
5. Coordinate the annual corporation/registration meeting in September
6. Make available at registration all the necessary student forms, and have the forms completed and filed for each student

PROGRAM

1. Supervise the day-to-day functioning of the program

2. Supervise curriculum development

3. Organize parties, programs, and any other special activities throughout the year

4. Handle any "Thank You" notes or proper acknowledgements needed for donations, volunteers, and the like

5. Inventory equipment and supplies at the beginning of the year and at midyear, and replace as needed

SPECIAL CONCERNS

1. Work with classroom teachers on any special needs of individual children

2. Maintain networking with other child care professionals, recommending to parents referrals to specialists as deemed necessary

3. Remain alert to signs of child abuse or neglect, reporting suspected cases as prescribed

FINANCES

1. Send out *Tuition Statements* or *Tuition Reminders* each month

2. Purchase all necessary supplies and snacks, and bring before the Board any requests for large equipment to be purchased from the equipment fund

3. Control the Teachers' Operating Fund, recording every purchase or charge, and furnishing to the Treasurer receipts and/or invoices for every purchase

BUSINESS

1. Keep parents informed and up-to-date on preschool policies, procedures, and activities through *Parent Newsletters* and notes posted at preschool

2. Attend all Board meetings to update the Board on all program happenings and concerns

3. Act as a liaison between the staff and Board

4. Publicize the preschool and maintain continuing public relations with the community

JOB DESCRIPTION—TEACHER

1. Supervise and insure the safety and well-being of the children at all times, being alert for the needs and/or problems of the children as individuals and as a group

2. Plan curriculum in detail for assigned classes, with team-teacher if applicable

3. Implement the daily program with the help of a team-teacher or aide if applicable

4. Arrange for field trips and write "Thank You" notes for trips

5. Decorate the room with bulletin boards, pictures, children's art work, and other hangings

6. Purchase or charge snacks and minor supplies, being reimbursed by the Director upon furnishing receipts

7. Prepare a snack for the children and sit with them while they eat it

8. Keep classroom, storage rooms, and bathroom clean, neat, and orderly

9. Conduct individual conferences with parents of each child at least twice yearly

10. Attend at least one continuing education seminar/workshop per school year

11. Be familiar with and follow all preschool policies

12. Keep Director informed in advance of program needs

13. Report to Director any special needs or problems of individual children

14. Report to Director any cases of suspected child abuse or neglect

15. Attend regular staff planning and evaluation meetings

16. Write and send home regular *Parent Newsletters*

17. Handle discipline promptly and in accordance with stated policy on discipline

JOB DESCRIPTION—TEACHER'S AIDE

1. Supervise and insure the safety and well-being of the children at all times, being alert for the needs and/or problems of the children as individuals and as a group

2. Assist assigned teacher in any way possible, which may include, but is not necessarily limited to:
   a. Plan curriculum in detail for assigned classes
   b. Implement the daily program for assigned classes
   c. Decorate the room with bulletin boards, pictures, children's art work, and other hangings
   d. Prepare a snack and sit with children while they eat it
   e. Keep classroom, storage rooms, and bathroom clean, neat, and orderly

3. Aides are encouraged to attend local in-service workshops

4. May assume temporary responsibilities of teacher in the absence of the teacher

5. Be familiar with and follow all preschool policies

6. Report to Director any special needs or problems of individual children

7. Report to Director any cases of suspected child abuse or neglect

8. Attend regular staff planning and evaluation meetings

JOB DESCRIPTION—
SUBSTITUTE TEACHER

1. Supervise and insure the safety and well-being of the children at all times, being alert for the needs and/or problems of the children as individuals and as a group

2. Curriculum

   a. Implement the daily program according to the lesson plans furnished by the regular teacher, *or*

   b. Assist assigned teacher in any way possible

3. Prepare a snack for the children and sit with them while they eat it

4. Keep classroom, storage rooms, and bathroom clean, neat, and orderly

5. Be familiar with and follow all procedural policies

6. Report to Director any special needs or problems of individual children

7. Report to Director any cases of suspected child abuse or neglect

8. Handle discipline promptly and in accordance with stated policy on discipline

JOB DESCRIPTION—SECRETARY

1. Keep attendance records

2. Keep registration records

3. Maintain all other preschool records as required

4. Receive visitors to, and phone calls about, the preschool

5. Send out information about the preschool as requested

6. Record minutes of organization meetings

7. Type and mail correspondence

8. Type and mail regular newsletters

9. Do typing, photocopying, and other office tasks as needed

10. Keep running inventory of office supplies and notify Director of needed supplies

JOB DESCRIPTION—BOOKKEEPER

1. Maintain staff employment records

2. Maintain payroll records, including vacations, sick leave, taxes, Social Security, worker's compensation, and any other deductions and benefits

3. File quarterly and year-end financial statements and pay corresponding taxes or fees

4. Issue payroll checks

5. Prepare and mail bills for tuition

6. Receive, record, and deposit tuition payments, donations, grants, and any other income

7. Order supplies and equipment as needed

8. Pay all bills and accounts

9. Keep precise records of all income and expenses

10. Report financial status regularly to governing body

FORM 2-11

STANDARDS

1. Be familiar with regulations regarding food service for program
2. Maintain standards of sanitation, health, safety, and nutrition
3. Attend continuing education as available and required
4. Supervise support staff as needed

FOOD PROCUREMENT

1. Inventory current supplies
2. Order or shop for needed items
3. Keep current records of inventory and expenses
4. Organize and maintain kitchen area
5. Order special foods as requested for classroom use, following specified procedures

FOOD PREPARATION

1. Plan menus, meeting requirements for nutrition
2. Post menus one month ahead
3. Prepare food
4. Prepare food for special functions, picnics, parties, and other functions, as needed

SERVING

1. Set tables
2. Serve food at designated times

CLEAN-UP

1. Clear tables immediately after meals
2. Wash dishes and utensils according to standards of sanitation
3. Properly handle and store leftover food

JOB DESCRIPTION—BUS DRIVER

STANDARDS

1. Meet requirements for training and licensing of drivers
2. Know current traffic laws
3. Attend continuing education as available and required

BUS PROCUREMENT

1. Make arrangements for use of bus if necessary
2. Check bus daily for fuel, and be sure everything is operational
3. Fill gas tank as needed, keeping accurate records of expenditures
4. Either do or arrange for regular routine maintenance
5. Keep bus neat and clean
6. If any problems occur, report to Director immediately

TRANSPORTING CHILDREN

1. Be sure children are aware of bus rules before boarding
2. Insure order and safety of children as they board and leave the bus
3. Maintain order and discipline on bus at all times
4. Keep an accurate count of children boarding and leaving bus
5. Be sure that each child is fastened in a safety device or seat belt before departure, and insist that they remain restrained while traveling
6. Insure that enough adults accompany the children so that the driver is free to devote all attention to safe driving

STANDARDS

1. Be familiar with standards regarding facility, maintenance, safety, and sanitation
2. Meet or exceed required standards
3. Maintain regular communication with Director
4. Meet with fire and sanitation inspectors for their regular licensing inspections

SUPPLIES

1. Inventory current supplies and equipment
2. Order or shop for needed items
3. Keep current records of inventory and expenses
4. Insure that all cleaning supplies and tools are safely locked out of the reach of children

CLEANING AND MAINTENANCE

1. Clean kitchen, bathrooms, classrooms, floors, and furniture regularly
2. Clean walls, carpet, hallways, and equipment, as needed
3. Launder children's linens regularly
4. Maintain building and equipment in safe and proper working order, checking periodically for hazards
5. Check fire extinguishers, fire alarms, smoke detectors, emergency and other safety equipment regularly to insure proper working order
6. Fulfill service requests as promptly as possible

RESPONSIBILITIES OF
THE BOARD OF DIRECTORS

SECURE STAFF FOR SCHOOL

1. Hire qualified Director, using state certification guidelines

2. Approve Director's hiring of teachers and aides

3. Issue staff *Contracts for Employment* by April 1 for following preschool year

4. Conduct annual evaluation of Director's performance, and participate in the evaluation of other staff

5. Make final decision on firing of staff

6. Operate within the preschool's personnel policies, updating those policies as required

MAINTAIN SCHOOL FINANCES

1. Approve following year's budget by March 31

2. Set tuition fees and salaries for the staff and Director annually

3. Apply for outside funding to provide for special needs

4. The treasurer's duties include:
   a. Collect tuition and deposit to preschool account
   b. Pay all bills, including salaries, taxes, and so on
   c. Pay monthly into teachers' operating fund
   d. Keep accurate records of all receipts and disbursements of funds

CONDUCT ALL OTHER NECESSARY BUSINESS

1. Give notice for and preside over annual meeting of the preschool corporation

2. Keep proper records of the meetings of the corporation and the Board of Directors

3. Elect officers and fill Board vacancies

4. Secure facilities for the preschool

5. Appoint committees as needed

6. Purchase insurance as necessary to cover preschool staff and Board

7. Oversee preschool operations

FORM 2-15

PARENTAL RESPONSIBILITIES

INFORMATION ON CHILD TO BE FILED BY THE FIRST WEEK OF CLASSES

1. Provide necessary information on registration forms
2. Insure that the child's immunizations are kept up-to-date, and provide the immunization information and physician's signature as required by state regulations

TUITION

1. Pay tuition either in full at the beginning of the year, or in equal monthly payments due by the 1st of each month
2. Payments made after the 15th of the month will be assessed a late fee

COMPLY WITH PROGRAM RULES AS DETAILED IN *PARENT INFORMATION BOOKLET*

1. Deliver and pick up child within times specified
2. Always leave the child with an adult
3. Keep child home when displaying signs of illness
4. Arrange to get child promptly if he/she becomes ill during school
5. Notify the school if the child has a communicable disease
6. Notify the school promptly of any planned changes in attendance
7. Attend conferences as scheduled to discuss child's progress

TAKE QUESTIONS OR PROBLEMS FIRST TO THE TEACHER CONCERNED. IF NOT RESOLVED CONTACT DIRECTOR, OR FINALLY, A BOARD MEMBER.

CONTRACT FOR EMPLOYMENT

Preschool _____

Employee Name _____

Address _____

_____

Phone _____ Social Security Number _____

This contract is between the above named Preschool and the above named Employee:

For the period beginning _____ and ending _____

For the position of _____

For the salary of _____

For the following hours per week _____

With the following stipulations _____

_____

Vacations _____

Sick leave _____

Personal leave _____

Insurance _____

Other benefits _____

_____

This contract is subject to the following documents, which are attached:

Job Description
Personnel Policies
Calendar of Holidays

_____   _____
Employer/Date   Employee/Date

© 1990 by The Center for Applied Research in Education, Inc.

FORM 2-17

EMPLOYEE TIME SHEET

Pay Period _____ through _____

Employee Name _____

Social Security Number _____ Position _____

Date	Time In	Time Out	Time In	Time Out	Leave Hours	Total Hours
				Total hours for pay period		

_____   _____
Employee's Signature   **Supervisor's Signature**

_____   _____
Date   **Date**

SUBSTITUTE TIME SHEET

Pay Period _____ through _____

Substitute Name _____

Mailing Address _____

Social Security Number _____ Phone _____

Substituted in what position _____

Date	Time In	Time Out	Time In	Time Out	Total Hours
				Total hours for pay period	

© 1990 by The Center for Applied Research in Education, Inc.

_____

Employee's Signature

_____

Supervisor's Signature

_____

Date

_____

Date

FORM 2-19

REQUEST FOR LEAVE

Name _____ Position _____

Type of leave requested

_____ Paid vacation

_____ Paid sick leave

_____ Paid personal leave

_____ Unpaid leave

Dates of requested leave _____ through _____

Reason for leave (optional) _____

_____

_____
Signature

_____
Date

****

Leave _____ approved or _____ denied

Comments _____

_____

_____

_____

_____
Signature

_____
Position

_____
Date

© 1990 by The Center for Applied Research in Education, Inc.

55

CRITERIA FOR
SELF-EVALUATION OF PROGRAM

PROGRAM CONTENT

Curriculum

Age Appropriate

Academics

Creative Outlets

Physical Activities

Music Appreciation

Use of Literature

Opportunities for Verbal Expression

Field Trips

Use of Outside Resources

Newsletters

FACILITY

Safe

Child-Oriented

Inviting

Attractive

Stimulating

Comfortable

Neat and Clean

Accessible

STAFF

Professional

Knowledgeable

Child-Oriented

Responsible

Prepared

Warm and caring

Open and Communicative

Helpful

Neat and clean

Cheerful

Fun

SNACKS/MEALS

Nutritious

Balanced

Tasty

Appealing

Frequency

Generous

New Taste Experiences

GENERAL

Cost

Registration Procedures

Conferences

Information Made Available to Parents

Opportunities for Parent Involvement

Efficiency of Total Operation

STAFF EVALUATION

Evaluation for _____
(Employee Name, Position)

For period beginning _____ and ending _____

    Please rate each item on a scale of 1–10, with 10 being "the best" and 1 being "the worst." Circle your choice.

Fulfillment of job obligations as stated in *Job Description* and *Contract for Employment*

    10   9   8   7   6   5   4   3   2   1

Compliance with state standards and regulations

    10   9   8   7   6   5   4   3   2   1

Compliance with objectives and goals as stated in the policies and as administered by the Director

    10   9   8   7   6   5   4   3   2   1

Physical, mental, and emotional competence to care for children

    10   9   8   7   6   5   4   3   2   1

Initiative in implementing the program

    10   9   8   7   6   5   4   3   2   1

Willingness to share the workload

    10   9   8   7   6   5   4   3   2   1

Relationship with other staff, Board, parents, and children

    10   9   8   7   6   5   4   3   2   1

Attendance and promptness

    10   9   8   7   6   5   4   3   2   1

Appropriate appearance and manner

    10   9   8   7   6   5   4   3   2   1

Dependability and reliability

    10   9   8   7   6   5   4   3   2   1

Total number of points: _____
(Maximum of 100)

* *

FORM 2-22

Result of staff evaluation by supervisor

_____ points of possible 100

Result of staff self-evaluation

_____ points of possible 100

Result of parent evaluation of program

_____ points of possible 420

_____ Working days in this evaluation period
_____ Sick days taken
_____ Vacation days taken
_____ Personal days taken

Recommendations: _____

_____

_____

_____

Supervisor's Signature, Position, and Date

I have completed a self-evaluation, and have read and discussed this evaluation with my supervisor.

_____

Employee's Signature

_____

Position

_____

Date

LETTER OF REFERENCE

(Your letterhead)

(Inside Address)

Dear   ,

As a part of our employment policies, our staff is involved in an annual evaluation process. The results of the most recent evaluation are reported below.

If you have any more specific questions about this employee, please contact

_____

Evaluation for _____

Date of evaluation _____

Result of staff evaluation by supervisor (based on a scale of 1 to 10, with 10 being the best):

_____ Fulfillment of job obligations

_____ Compliance with state standards

_____ Compliance with objectives and goals

_____ Competence to care for children

_____ Initiative

_____ Willingness to share workload

_____ Relationship with others

_____ Attendance and promptness

_____ Appropriate appearance and manner

_____ Dependability and reliability

Result of staff evaluation by supervisor

_____ points of possible 100

Result of staff self-evaluation

_____ points of possible 100

Result of parent evaluation of employees portion of program

_____ points of possible 420

_____ Working days in this evaluation period

_____ Sick days taken

_____ Vacation days taken

_____ Personal days taken

© 1990 by The Center for Applied Research in Education, Inc.

FORM 2-23

Recommendations _____

_____

_____

_____

_____

_____

_____

_____

_____

_____

_____

_____

Supervisor's Signature

_____   _____

Position   **Date**

AWARD
FOR
EXCELLENCE

IS PRESENTED THIS
AWARD
FOR EXCELLENCE IN

EMPLOYEE COMPLAINT

Submitted by _____

Nature of complaint _____

_____

_____

_____

_____

_____

_____

Has this same thing happened before? _____   If so, when? _____

Documented? _____

_____

Employee's Signature

_____

Date

****

SUPERVISOR FOLLOW-UP

Was any action taken on this matter? _____   If so, what? _____

_____

_____

_____

_____

Supervisor's Signature

_____

Date

DOCUMENTATION OF EMPLOYMENT PROBLEM

Name of employee _____

Report submitted by _____

Nature of complaint _____

_____

_____

_____

_____

_____

Has this same thing happened before? _____ If so, when? _____

Documented? _____

Were there any witnesses? _____ If so, witness's comments here: _____

_____

_____

_____

_____

_____

Was employee made aware of this problem? _____ If so, what were the results?

_____

_____

_____

_____

_____

Was there any further action? _____ If so, what? _____

_____

_____

_____

_____

_____

_____

Signature/Position

_____

Date

SUPERVISOR/STAFF CONFERENCE

Date _____

Conference called by _____

Reason for conference _____

_____

_____

_____

_____

_____

STAFF MEMBER

This is my understanding of our conversation:

_____

_____

_____

_____

_____

_____

_____

_____

_____

                                           _____
Signature/Date

SUPERVISOR

This is my understanding of our conversation:

_____

_____

_____

_____

_____

_____

_____

_____

                                           _____
Signature/Date

CERTIFICATE OF TRAINING

Name _____

Address _____

_____

Attended _____ hours of training

Sponsored by _____

Location _____

_____

Training topic _____

Presented by _____

Of _____

Date of Training _____

Authorized Signature _____

- -

CERTIFICATE OF TRAINING

Name _____

Address _____

_____

Attended _____ hours of training

Sponsored by _____

Location _____

_____

Training topic _____

Presented by _____

Of _____

Date of Training _____

Authorized Signature _____

RECORD OF CONTINUING EDUCATION

Name _____

Date	Training Program	Sponsored By	Instructor	Hours

EVALUATION OF TRAINING

Name of training program _____

Presented by _____ Date _____

Report by _____

Did you attend _____ alone _____ with other staff

_____ with others from the community

Did you attend _____ during working hours _____ after working hours

_____ on the weekend

Were you paid for your time? _____ yes , _____ no

Were you reimbursed for your expenses? _____ yes _____ no

Was the material _____ new _____ review _____ outdated

Was the training well presented? _____ yes _____ no

_____

Content: Was the information presented

_____ too much _____ too little _____ just enough

_____

Was the information applicable to our preschool? _____

_____

Was the information age-appropriate? _____

_____

Was the program inspiring? _____

_____

Was the program worth your time? _____

_____

Was the program worth our expense? _____

_____

Would you recommend this training to a colleague? _____

Why or why not? _____

Additional comments _____

_____

_____

_____

_____

_____

_____

_____

_____

_____

VOUCHER FOR TRAVEL EXPENSES

Employee name _____

Travel period _____ through _____

Travel to _____

For _____

Date	Miles	Registration Fee	Meals	Room	Other Expenses

PLEASE ATTACH ALL RECEIPTS

_____   _____
Employee's Signature/Date   Supervisor's Signature/Date

•••

The following totals are approved for reimbursement:

Mileage	Registration Fee	Meals	Room	Other Expenses

_____
Authorized Signature/Date

REGISTRATION MATERIALS

This section consists of forms used in the registration process. The format used throughout this section is that used by a preschool program operating on a nine-month academic year; therefore a mass registration meeting is held once per year in the fall. For a twelve-month continuous program, most of the same forms could be used, but there would be no mass registration meeting once per year.

3–1 Sample Procedure for Registration Meeting outlines the procedure used for the annual registration meeting. It is a guideline for the staff in preparing for the meeting, and will need to be tailored to fit your program and registration needs.

3–2 Registration Checklist is completed for each class with the names of the preregistered children and their parent information. It is then used at the registration meeting to confirm the accuracy of the child's identifying information and to record payment of tuition and fees. As the various registration forms come in, this checklist is used again to record which forms have been received and which forms have yet to be received.

3–3 Sample Registration Letter is an example of the information sent to the parents of each of the preregistered children inviting them to the registration meeting. This letter should detail preschool class days and times, as well as tuition and any additional fees.

3–4 Preregistration Form is the method of recording the information on children who are asking to be enrolled in the preschool. In a nine-month program, this form may be sent home with each of the children attending in the spring of the year so that they may be the first ones to return it and register for the following fall. These forms are then kept in a three-ring binder: the completed forms under the appropriate class, and the blank ones ready to be completed as registrations are called in. When you are then ready to register the child for a class, this information is used to place children and to send additional information to the parent.

3–5/6 Parent Information Booklet Outline and Sample offer a brief outline of the materials that should be included in the actual parent booklet, along with an example of how one program presents parent information. The text is printed on both sides of white paper such that it can be folded in half and stapled in the center to form a $5\frac{1}{2} \times 8\frac{1}{2}$-inch booklet. The cover can be color-coded in the color for registration materials and decorated by the preschool logo. This booklet and the remaining forms in this chapter constitute the new-child packet, which is distributed at the registration meeting.

3–7 Registration Form contains the information about each child that is to be on file at the preschool. It should be the first form in each child's file folder. If children remain enrolled in your program from one year to the next, it would be advisable to have the parent complete a new registration form each year to update the information.

3–8 Enrollment Form for Child with Special Needs is to be used in addition to the *Registration Form* for children who need special planning and support services. This form is to be completed by a professional working with the child, preferably one who is willing to be on the planning and evaluation team supporting the child for the preschool year.

3–9 Permission for Health Care is to be complete and on file for each child. This form too should be redone each year to remain current.

3–10 Field Trip Permission Form is the preliminary permission for taking the child on field trips during the year. It is an understanding with the parent that field trips are important and that the child will be allowed to participate. It gives the parent the option of bringing a personal child safety device for use by his/her child. It also informs the parent that, for each trip, an information and permission form will be provided so that the parent may decide with each trip whether to grant or deny permission.

3–11 Sample Parent's Page asks for parent participation and support for the program. It also asks for help in developing a community resources file, which can be used for curriculum enhancement.

3–12 Permission for Screening asks for parental permission to conduct the routine developmental screening done for each child by the preschool staff. If problems are found, they are reported to the parent on the *Child Concern Letter*.

3–13 Dental Card can be made up on a half sheet. It is to be completed by the child's dentist in an effort to encourage regular dental care.

3–14 Sample Calendar of Holidays informs the parents, as well as the staff, of the holidays during the year when the preschool will not be in session.

3–15 Sample School Calendar can be used alone or with the *Sample Calendar of Holidays* to inform parents and staff of special days throughout the year. Any changes in the calendar can be made through the weekly *Parent Newsletter*.

SAMPLE PROCEDURE FOR REGISTRATION MEETING

I. Notice of registration to current students in April; parents may register and pay fees at that time

II. Plan registration meeting to be held for the following purposes:
   A. Guarantee the child's place in the class
   B. Complete registration
   C. Pick up required registration forms
   D. Receive calendar and other important information
   E. Discuss registration materials and go over policies
   F. Ask any questions parents may have
   G. Pay fees
   H. Meet staff and Board
   I. See classrooms
   J. Election of Board of Directors for the coming year

III. Set up for registration meeting
   A. Send registration letter to parents by August 15 informing them that:
      1. Each child must have at least one parent in attendance to complete registration or the child's place in the class is forfeited to a paying parent—unless prior arrangements have been made
      2. Parents pay fees at registration meeting unless prior arrangements have been made
   B. Hold registration meeting on Monday of week before classes begin
   C. Have registration materials ready at door and Director at door to give out materials and direct parents to proper classroom
      1. *Parent Information Booklet* (yellow cover)
      2. *Registration Form* (yellow)—have parent complete and leave at registration meeting
      3. *Field Trip Permission Form* (pale yellow)
      4. *Permission for Health Care* (blue)—be sure another authorized adult is listed
      5. *Record of Immunization Card* (dark blue)—obtained from Human Services (contact early)
      6. *Dental Card* (pale blue)
      7. *Parent's Page* (goldenrod)
      8. *Permission for Screening* (orange)
      9. *School Calendar* (white)
   D. Have classrooms set up with one Board member per room to take tuition and fees, and one teacher per room to talk with parents
   E. Have *Registration Checklists* in each room completed with children's names and parent information
   F. Have parents check existing information for accuracy
   G. Complete the checklist as tuition and fees are paid and materials are returned
   H. Stay with the time schedule
      6:20—Everything and everybody ready
      6:30—Registrations begin
      6:45—Introductions and discussion of materials
      7:15—Election of Board members
      7:45—Complete registrations
   I. Have refreshments available to encourage conversation

FORM 3-1

REGISTRATION CHECKLIST

Registration form								Child's Name Birthdate	Address Parent's Name	Phone
Immunization form										
Permission for health care										
Field trip release										
Parent's page										
Screening										
Check										
Cash										

SAMPLE REGISTRATION LETTER

(Your letterhead)

August 15, 19 _____

Dear Parents,

We would like to welcome you and your children to Hillside Preschool; which is now in its 30th year of operation. We are looking forward to an exciting new year with your children.

Classes will begin on September 3 and end on May 23. Our 3-year-old classes meet from 9:00 to 11:00 two mornings per week. Our 4-year-old classes meet from 9:00 to 11:30 three mornings per week.

Tuition for 3-year-old classes is $ _315_ for the year, or, if you prefer, it may be paid in nine monthly installments of $ _35/_ by the first of each month. Tuition for 4-year-old classes is $ _405_ for the year, or it may be paid in nine monthly installments of $ _45/_ by the first of each month. For each child there is a $ _____ equipment fee, due once per year, payable at registration.

Registration will be completed at a parent meeting on Monday, August 26 from 6:30 to 7:45 P.M. in the downstairs meeting room of St. Peter's Episcopal Church. This meeting will be your time to pick up registration forms, pay your fees to insure your child's place in the class, talk to other parents about carpools, meet the Board and staff, discuss registration forms and preschool policies, and elect a Board of Directors for the current year. It is extremely important that you attend this meeting in order to insure your child's place in the class.

This is also the annual meeting of the Hillside Preschool Corporation, of which you will be a paying member. An election will be held to fill the vacancies on the Board of Directors for the coming year. Please consider accepting a position on the Board yourself, or supporting another father or mother who may be willing to serve. Come prepared to volunteer or to nominate someone else, for this is your preschool, and your opportunity to have a hand in directing its operation.

We look forward to seeing you on the 26th of August. Come prepared to pay your tuition and equipment fee, elect a Board of Directors, pick up registration forms, and have your questions answered.

Sincerely,

Hillside Preschool Board and Staff

PREREGISTRATION FORM

Today's date _____   Registration number _____

Child's name _____   Nickname _____

Age on September 1 _____   Sex _____   Birthdate _____

Name of parent or guardian with whom child lives _____

Mailing address _____

Phone _____

Days preferred: 4-year-olds _____ MWF _____ TThF

               3-year-olds _____ MTh _____ TTh

Is there any child you especially want to attend with? _____

_____

- -

PREREGISTRATION FORM

Today's date _____   Registration number _____

Child's name _____   Nickname _____

Age on September 1 _____   Sex _____   Birthdate _____

Name of parent or guardian with whom child lives _____

Mailing address _____

Phone _____

Days preferred: 4-year-olds _____ MWF _____ TThF

               3-year-olds _____ MTh _____ TTh

Is there any child you especially want to attend with? _____

_____

PARENT INFORMATION BOOKLET OUTLINE

    I. PROGRAM

    II. STANDARDS

    III. INCORPORATION

    IV. AFFIRMATIVE ACTION STATEMENT

    V. ADMISSIONS

    VI. LOCATION

    VII. DAYS AND HOURS OF OPERATION

    VIII. PICK-UP AND DELIVERY OF CHILDREN

    IX. TUITION

    X. HEALTH INFORMATION

    XI. DRESS

    XII. FIELD TRIPS

    XIII. SNACKS

    XIV. DISCIPLINE

    XV. CONFIDENTIALITY OF RECORDS

    XVI. WITHDRAWAL

    XVII. COMMUNICATION WITH PARENTS

    XVIII. CURRENT BOARD OF DIRECTORS

    XIX. CURRENT STAFF

FORM 3-5

PROGRAM

It is the philosophy of Hillside Preschool that early childhood should be a time of fun, warmth, security, exploring, and discovery. Preschool children are creative and receptive; the staff strives to nurture and encourage these qualities in the children who attend.

The preschool's purpose is to provide an atmosphere that encourages social, emotional, physical, and intellectual growth and development of the child as a whole.

Planned within the framework of philosophy and purpose, Hillside Preschool's curriculum includes sharing and conversation time; stories, songs, and fingerplays; creative art activities and crafts; games and large muscle activities; field trips throughout the community; food preparation; science and nature activities; exposure to shapes, colors, numbers, and letters; and celebration of birthdays and holidays.

STANDARDS

Hillside Preschool, established in 1960, is licensed by this state's Department of Public Assistance and Social Services, and complies with all of the standards put forth by that Department. Its operation is governed by a volunteer Board of Directors and a paid Director. Each class is taught by at least one degreed teacher.

INCORPORATION

Hillside Preschool is a nonprofit corporation, and the parents of children registered for the current school year form the membership of the corporation. An annual meeting is held in September, at which time new members are elected to the Board of Directors from the corporate membership. Each parent has one vote for a maximum of two votes per family unit in electing Board members.

Incorporation protects the individual Board and staff members against liability in carrying out their respective duties.

AFFIRMATIVE ACTION STATEMENT

Hillside Preschool advertises in the public media in order to make openings known to all. Children are admitted regardless of race, creed, color, sex, national origin, or religion. Handicapped children will be accepted on the approval of the instructor, Director, and Board.

ADMISSIONS

Children who are 3 years old up to kindergarten age are eligible to enroll in the preschool. Admission requirements and enrollment procedures are as follows:

1. A child must be 3 years old by September 1 to be admitted into the 3-year-old class.
2. Children in the 3-year-old class will not be allowed to advance into the 4-year-old class during the school year.
3. A child must be 4 years old by September 1 to be admitted into the 4-year-old class.

4. If a parent intends to enroll a child in kindergarten before the standard age of 5, and if the parent can provide written verification by the school system that the child will be attending kindergarten the following school year, then the child may be enrolled in the 4-year-old class.

5. Classes are filled on a first-come/first-served basis according to the date of enrollment with the Director.

6. If the clases are filled when a parent calls, the child's name will be put on a waiting list to fill vacancies as they occur.

7. Parents of enrolled children receive a letter in the fall inviting them to the registration meeting where registration is completed.

8. As vacancies occur during the year, they are filled from the waiting list, or from new registrations, according to the above procedures.

LOCATION

Hillside Preschool is located in the basement of St. Peter's Episcopal Church, 1 South Main Street. Please use the entrance at the south end of the building near the flag pole.

DAYS AND HOURS OF OPERATION

The preschool is open from the first Tuesday after Labor Day until the last Friday before Memorial Day
    Three-year-old classes contain a maximum of fifteen children, and meet two days per week from 9:00 to 11:00 A.M.
    Four-year-old classes contain a maximum of eighteen children, and meet three days per week from 9:00 to 11:30 A.M.
    Hillside Preschool follows the public school yearly calendar, closing for the same holidays and vacations. Because of the state regulations concerning class size and teacher ratio, missed days may not be made up on nonscheduled days.
    Hillside Preschool also follows the public school's emergency closing procedures. If public school is dismissed early because of weather conditions, preschool will close at the same time. Listen to the local radio station for early closing information.

PICK-UP AND DELIVERY OF CHILDREN

No child is to be brought to preschool more than 10 minutes before class begins, nor picked up more than 10 minutes after class is over. If a child is left beyond those limits with no arrangements made, a babysitting fee will be assessed when the child is picked up.
    For safety's sake, children must always be left in the care of an adult, with the children being brought directly to the classroom. Children must never be left at preschool without a teacher present. Parents are asked to return to the classroom to pick up their children after class is over.

TUITION

Tuition is figured as an annual fee. It may be paid in full at registration, or in nine equal monthly installments due on the first of each month, beginning with September and ending with May. Because tuition is an annual fee, no refunds are given for illness, vacations, or snow days, and those days are not made up.

© 1990 by The Center for Applied Research in Education, Inc.

At registration the first tuition payment is due, as well as the annual equipment fee, which is paid by each child regardless of arrangements made for payment of tuition.

It is very important that tuition be paid on time. In the event that tuition payments are late, parents will be given up to one month to make restitution. Hillside preschool reserves the right to assess an additional charge of up to 10 percent (10%) of the amount of past-due tuition. If, after one month, payment has not been made, the parents will be asked to withdraw their child from preschool, and further action will be taken against the parents.

If the parents are unable to pay tuition due to economic conditions, they may apply to the Board for consideration for the scholarship fund. Applications for scholarship funds will be considered on a case-by-case basis by the Board.

HEALTH INFORMATION

Each child is required by state regulations to have on file a health statement, which includes a record of up-to-date immunizations and the signature of the child's source of medical care. If a child's health care summary is not complete at the time of enrollment or within thirty (30) days after enrollment, the child will be excluded from the program.

Each child who has not had a physical examination within the last year must have one before entrance into preschool. This physical may be done by a physician, public health nurse, or preschool screening clinic.

The preschool must have on file for each child a signed *Permission for Health Care* authorizing emergency care and transfer of medical records to the local hospital. Emergency numbers for reaching the parent or guardian and another authorized person must also be on file.

No child who arrives at preschool noticeably ill, with a rash, or with a fever will be admitted for that day. Should a child become ill during the day, the parent is notified immediately. The child is taken to the sick room and remains there under adult supervision until the parent or authorized person arrives to take the child home.

In the event a child contracts a communicable disease and exposes the other children, notice of such exposure will be posted, and parents will be notified when they pick up their children. The ill child will not be allowed to return to preschool until the period of contagion has passed.

In case of medical emergency during a preschool session, first aid will be administered by the staff. The parent or authorized adult will be notified as quickly as possible. If medical attention is required, the staff will call the local ambulance service, who will transport the child to the local hospital. Every effort will be made to contact the child's own physician.

DRESS

Children are encouraged to wear play clothes and tennis shoes. Daily activities include active and messy play, and the children should feel comfortable enough to enjoy themselves without worrying about their clothes. The child's name should be placed on all outdoor clothing and other belongings to help ensure the return of all the proper possessions and clothes.

Special preschool logo t-shirts are available for parents to purchase for their child. The staff encourages the children to wear their t-shirts on all field trips and outings.

FIELD TRIPS

An important part of Hillside Preschool's curriculum is exposing the children to many and varied experiences within the community; therefore a number of field trips are built into the preschool year.

Parents will be informed of field trips in advance through newsletters and a permission form sent home for each trip. Parents are frequently asked to drive for field trips. The requirements for drivers are that they carry only the number of children they can buckle into individual seat belts, and that their insurance coverage be current.

SNACKS

The preschool furnishes snacks for the children each morning. Snacks are used as a part of the curriculum, often related to the unit topic, and as an experience in tasting. Parents are asked to provide their children with breakfast before coming to preschool.

With advance notice children may bring special treats for their birthday or any other time during the preschool year. Because of state regulations regarding the serving of food, the treats must be purchased commercially, either prepackaged or from a bakery.

DISCIPLINE

Acceptable behavior is encouraged by giving positive verbal rewards. This reinforces a child's good feeling about his/her behavior and serves as an example to the other children to act in such a way as to receive this praise. Asking a child to stop and think about his/her unpleasant behavior enables that child to work at self-control.

For a child not cooperating in a group listening situation, the child is seated by a teacher and reminded of acceptable behavior.

Removal from the group for a period of time-out is the next tactic used for a child who continually demonstrates unacceptable behavior. This time-out is not a punishment, but rather a time when the child may calm down, remember what behavior the teacher is asking for, and decide for him- or herself when he/she is ready to rejoin the group with appropriate behavior.

Corporal punishment is not considered to be an accepted method of dealing with young children's behavior. Children will not be hit, slapped, or spanked in any manner while attending Hillside Preschool.

If behavior problems persist, the parent is asked to a conference to discuss what may be helpful in motivating the child to behave in an acceptable way. It may be suggested that the child be involved in a behavior modification program, with the parent having the option of being involved in the process as well.

CONFIDENTIALITY OF RECORDS

Children's records are open only to the child's teacher, the Director, an authorized employee of the licensing agency, or the child's parent or legal guardian.

WITHDRAWAL

If a child needs to be withdrawn from preschool, two weeks notice is required so that the vacancy can be filled by another child. Should more notice be possible, it would be appreciated.

COMMUNICATIONS WITH PARENTS

This booklet has been supplied in an effort to answer many of your questions. Please contact anyone on the staff or Board if you have more questions.

FORM 3-6

Parents are informed of the activities of the preschool through weekly newsletters. The newsletter includes weekly unit topics, class activities, field trips, and suggestions for parents.

Two parent conferences are offered during the year, one in the fall and one in the spring. Either the parent or the teacher may request an additional conference any time there is a special concern.

Because of state regulations concerning class size and teacher ratio, it is not possible for children to bring friends to visit.

Parents are encouraged to visit preschool at any time. Because of occasional field trips and special activities, advance notice is suggested. If the teachers are not free to talk with you, please understand that the children come first during class time; the teachers will be happy to talk with you after the children are dismissed. Please remember that this is your preschool and your child's education. So come and find out what is happening!

CURRENT BOARD OF DIRECTORS

[Names]

CURRENT STAFF

[Names]

REGISTRATION FORM

Child's full name _____

Name child goes by _____

Date of birth _____ Sex _____

Child's home address _____

_____

Child's home phone number _____

PARENT OR GUARDIAN INFORMATION

Father's name _____ Phone _____

Father's address _____

Father's occupation and place of employment _____

_____ Phone _____

Mother's name _____ Phone _____

Mother's address _____

Mother's occupation and place of employment _____

_____ Phone _____

FAMILY INFORMATION

Brothers and/or sisters (please indicate ages and whether they live with the child)

_____

_____

_____

_____

_____

Please list any other persons living with the child and their relationship (if any) to the child

_____

_____

PICK-UP

Persons authorized to pick up child _____

_____

_____

Persons who *may not* pick up child _____

_____

_____

PERSONAL HISTORY

Is child right-handed or left-handed? _____

Has child had a previous group or preschool experience? _____

    If so, where and when? _____

_____

Does child have any allergies? _____

_____

Are there any medical problems of which we should be aware? _____

_____

What words does child use for toileting? _____

_____

Does child have any bowel or bladder irregularities? _____

_____

Are there any special food or eating instructions? _____

_____

Are there any sleeping or napping instructions? _____

_____

Any additional information such as discipline, child's communication, comforting, and so on?

_____

_____

_____

_____

_____

_____

_____

_____

_____

_____

_____

_____

_____

_____

_____

_____

ENROLLMENT FORM FOR CHILD WITH SPECIAL NEEDS

Child's name _____

Parent's name _____

Name of physician or therapist _____

    Address _____

    _____

    Phone number _____

Diagnosis of child's condition _____
_____

Simple explanation of how the condition affects the child's care and/or education
_____
_____
_____
_____

Special instructions _____
_____
_____
_____
_____
_____

Who should be involved in planning and evaluation for this child? _____
_____
_____

How often should a follow-up evaluation of progess be done? _____
_____

_____
(Form completed by/Position/Date)

FORM 3-8

PERMISSION FOR HEALTH CARE

Child's name _____ Date _____

Child's physician _____ Phone _____

    Address _____

Child's dentist _____ Phone _____

    Address _____

AUTHORIZED ADULTS

In the event of an emergency, please indicate your name and phone number where you and another authorized person can be reached.

Father's name _____ Phone _____

Mother's name _____ Phone _____

Another authorized person _____ Phone _____

    Address _____

FIRST AID

In the event of an emergency, I authorize the staff to provide any first aid care deemed necessary for my child.

_____
Signature/Date

EMERGENCY CARE

In the event of an emergency in which I cannot be reached, the physician listed above and the local hospital are hereby authorized to provide any emergency care deemed necessary for my child.

_____
Signature/Date

HEALTH RECORD TRANSFER

In the event of an emergency, I hereby authorize the transfer of my child's health record to the local hospital.

_____
Signature/Date

© 1990 by The Center for Applied Research in Education, Inc.

FIELD TRIP PERMISSION FORM

Child's name _____ Date _____

I understand that field trips are an integral part of the curriculum, and that I will be asked permission for each field trip as it approaches. I further understand that my child will be secured in a seat belt or child safety device while being transported in a car on a field trip. With this understanding, I hereby give my permission for the staff and volunteers of Hillside Preschool to take my child on field trips while he/she is in the program.

_____
Parent's Signature/Date

My child is too young and/or too small to use a seat belt, therefore I assume responsibility for providing a suitable child safety device for my child to use on field trips.

_____
Parent's Signature/Date

– –

FIELD TRIP PERMISSION FORM

Child's name _____ Date _____

I understand that field trips are an integral part of the curriculum, and that I will be asked permission for each field trip as it approaches. I further understand that my child will be secured in a seat belt or child safety device while being transported in a car on a field trip. With this understanding, I hereby give my permission for the staff and volunteers of Hillside Preschool to take my child on field trips while he/she is in the program.

_____
Parent's Signature/Date

My child is too young and/or too small to use a seat belt, therefore I assume responsibility for providing a suitable child safety device for my child to use on field trips.

_____
Parent's Signature/Date

FORM 3-10

SAMPLE PARENT'S PAGE

Parents are a vital part of Hillside Preschool: parents are the membership of the corporation; parents elect and serve on the Board of Directors; parents provide financial support; and parents can be of great support in other ways as well.

In order to take field trips, we need to take enough vehicles so that each child can be safely buckled into a seat belt or child safety device. Therefore we ask if we may call upon you on occasion to drive for a field trip.

Another way that parents can enhance our program is by helping with parties and other special occasions. So we ask if we may call upon you to help with a special occasion.

Every family can help by saving containers for our use. Jar lids of all kinds can be used as paint containers, and we use many kinds of ice cream buckets and margarine tubs. These may be sent with your child at any time throughout the year.

We also ask for your help in compiling a "Community Resources File." We strive to expose the children to many varied experiences. We would appreciate any ideas you may have as to places we could take the children, or people who could come in to share their special hobby, skill, or collection. Whatever might interest children and increase their awareness of the world around them is appropriate.

Please detach the bottom of this form and, after much consideration, return it to the teachers. Thank you for your part in helping to make Hillside Preschool a valuable experience for our community's young children.

* *

PARENT'S PAGE

Child's name _____

Parent's name _____

Please indicate if you are able to:
    Drive for field trips   Father _____   Mother _____
    Help with special occasions   Father _____   Mother _____

COMMUNITY RESOURCES FILE

What to see _____

Person to contact _____

Address _____ Phone _____

PERMISSION FOR SCREENING

As a service to the children of Hillside Preschool, our staff does a routine developmental screening of each new child. The child's speech and language, gross motor (large muscles) and fine motor (small muscles), cognitive and social skills are screened, along with a vision and hearing check. This is not a medical checkup, and will not tell us how smart your child is. It will tell us whether your child is functioning within normal limits compared to other children of the same age.

If you have any specific concerns or questions regarding your child's development, please list below:

_____

_____

Child's name _____ Birthdate _____

I give my permission for my child to receive a developmental screening by the preschool staff. I understand that I will be informed of the results.

_____
Parent's Signature/Date

- -

PERMISSION FOR SCREENING

As a service to the children of Hillside Preschool, our staff does a routine developmental screening of each new child. The child's speech and language, gross motor (large muscles) and fine motor (small muscles), cognitive and social skills are screened, along with a vision and hearing check. This is not a medical checkup, and will not tell us how smart your child is. It will tell us whether your child is functioning within normal limits compared to other children of the same age.

If you have any specific concerns or questions regarding your child's development, please list below:

_____

_____

Child's name _____ Birthdate _____

I give my permission for my child to receive a developmental screening by the preschool staff. I understand that I will be informed of the results.

_____
Parent's Signature/Date

DENTAL CARD

Child's name _____

I have performed an oral examination for this child and have informed his/her parents of all necessary dental treatment.

Is in treatment _____ Treatment completed _____

_____
Signature/Date

....

DENTAL CARD

Child's name _____

I have performed an oral examination for this child and have informed his/her parents of all necessary dental treatment.

Is in treatment _____ Treatment completed _____

_____
Signature/Date

....

DENTAL CARD

Child's name _____

I have performed an oral examination for this child and have informed his/her parents of all necessary dental treatment.

Is in treatment _____ Treatment completed _____

_____
Signature/Date

....

DENTAL CARD

Child's name _____

I have performed an oral examination for this child and have informed his/her parents of all necessary dental treatment.

Is in treatment _____ Treatment completed _____

_____
Signature/Date

FORM 3-13

THERE WILL BE NO CLASSES ON THE FOLLOWING HOLIDAYS.

Please mark your calendar.

September 2	Labor Day
November 11	Veterans Day
November 28–December 1	Thanksgiving Vacation
December 19–January 1	Winter Vacation
January 15	Martin Luther King Day
February 16	Presidents Day
April 4–7	Spring Vacation
May 26	Memorial Day

SAMPLE PRESCHOOL CALENDAR

August 26	Monday	Registration Meeting
September 3	Tuesday	School Begins
October 31	Thursday	Halloween Party
November 11–12	Monday–Tuesday	Conferences
November 28–December 1	Thursday–Sunday	Thanksgiving Vacation
December 18	Wednesday	Holiday Party
December 19–January 1	Thursday–Wednesday	Winter Vacation
February 14	Friday	Valentine Party
April 4–7	Friday–Monday	Spring Vacation
April 20–26	Sunday–Saturday	Week of the Young Child
May 5–6	Monday–Tuesday	Conferences
May 19	Monday	Skating Party
May 23	Friday	Last Day of School

PARENT-TEACHER CONFERENCES

The forms in this section have to do with conferences or communication with parents. Some of the forms are for routine conferences, which are offered regularly to all parents, while others are meant for special concerns and circumstances.

4–1 Suggestions for Conferences is a list of ideas to get you started when planning conferences with parents. The same suggestions apply whether it is a routine conference, or one precipitated by a special concern.

4–2 Parent-Teacher Conferences is the form to be sent home with the children to get an indication of a convenient time for the parents to attend a conference. Appropriate conference days and times should be completed in the first paragraph by the teacher; the parent will then complete the form and send it back to the teacher.

4–3 Conference Confirmation is completed on a quarter-page and is sent home with each child to inform the parent of the specific time and date reserved for that child's conference.

4–4 All About Me is intended to be a simple, objective evaluation of where the child falls in relation to the expectations of the preschool and/or staff, and also in relation to other children of the same age. A checkmark in the "I can" or "I need help" column is all that is required. The same form may be used in the fall marked in black pencil, and again in the spring marked in red to indicate progress. A copy may be sent home with the parent at the fall conference, and the original given to the parent in the spring. A copy should be kept in the child's file.

4–5 Kindergarten Entrance Skills is a guideline for assessing the skills often expected to be developed by the time a child leaves preschool and enters kindergarten. It is meant to be a tool to use in discussing kindergarten readiness with parents at the spring conference. The original is to go to the parent, and a copy kept in the child's file.

4–6 Individualized Plan for Child with Special Needs is the companion form to go with *Enrollment Form For Child With Special Needs*. It is a record of the educational plan developed by the child's support team, and a proposal for the evaluation of the child's progress within the plan. The original should be kept at school, and a copy given to the parent and each member of the team.

4–7 Documentation of Concern for a Child records any concern about a child and documentation supporting that concern. This form is meant to be discussed, acted upon, and then kept in the child's file.

4–8 Child Concern Letter is a letter sent to the parent of a child about which there is a particular concern. It briefly outlines the concern and sets up a time for the parent to visit with the teacher about that concern.

4–9 Permission for Further Evaluation asks specifically for the parent's permission for further evaluation of the child. It is to be used at the conference with the parent, after discussing the concern and the purpose for the further evaluation.

4–10 Child Award is an award given to a child for a special accomplishment. It could be a part of a behavior modification plan, something that is done for each child on a regular basis for positive reinforcement, or just something extra on a special occasion.

4–11 Record of Conferences is a concise record of conferences offered and whether the parents took advantage of the opportunity. The same form may be kept in the child's file the entire time he/she is in the program.

SUGGESTIONS FOR CONFERENCES

TIMING

1. Do not rob children of attention to talk to parents.
   a. Get another adult to tend to children.
   b. Ask parents to come back when you can give them your full attention.

2. Never discuss a child in his/her presence, unless you are talking *to* that child.
   a. Specifically ask parents not to bring children to conferences.
   b. Have a separate playroom set up or a headset and tapes for a child who does show up.

3. Allow yourself enough time to set the parent at ease and be able to cover the intended topic, but do not allow for irrelevant chatter.
   a. 15 minutes may not be long enough for a conference.
   b. 30 minutes may be too long.

WHAT TO SAY

1. Know what you are going to say to the parent.
   a. Have notes, evaluation forms, test results, and such available, as concrete as possible.
   b. As far as possible, provide the parent with facts, examples, quotes, samples, and so on.

2. Make your comments as constructive and positive as possible.

3. If you need to discuss a behavior you do not like, be sure you emphasize that it is the *behavior,* and not the child, that you dislike.

4. Offer the parents suggestions as to what they could do to be involved in the education process.

5. Take time to listen to what the parents have to say—you can learn much about the child from what the parents share.

6. Solicit the parents' help and suggestions on how to deal with problem behaviors.

7. Make available to parents as much information as you can about what happens at school by writing newsletters, posting menus, encouraging visitation, offering conferences, allowing parents to help if interested.

8. End conferences on a positive note.

PARENT-TEACHER CONFERENCES

Parent-teacher conferences will be held on _____ .

Conferences will be scheduled for 20-minute intervals between the hours of 8:00 A.M. and 1:00 P.M., and again between 7:00 P.M. and 9:00 P.M.

Please indicate below your choice of conference time. We will then notify you as to the exact time we have reserved for you

Since this is a time for us to discuss your child's progress, and since we will not discuss a child in his/her presence, please make other arrangements for your child. We will make every effort to stay within the time schedule.

_____ I can come at any time.

_____ I can come in the morning.

_____ I can come during my lunch hour, which is from _____ to _____ .

_____ If possible I prefer an evening appointment, but I can come at the other times indicated.

_____ Evening is the only time I can come.

_____   _____
Child's Name   **Parent's Signature**

- -

PARENT-TEACHER CONFERENCES

Parent-teacher conferences will be held on _____ .

Conferences will be scheduled for 20-minute intervals between the hours of 8:00 A.M. and 1:00 P.M., and again between 7:00 P.M. and 9:00 P.M.

Please indicate below your choice of conference time. We will then notify you as to the exact time we have reserved for you.

Since this is a time for us to discuss your child's progress, and since we will not discuss a child in his/her presence, please make other arrangements for your child. We will make every effort to stay within the time schedule.

_____ I can come at any time.

_____ I can come in the morning.

_____ I can come during my lunch hour, which is from _____ to _____ .

_____ If possible I prefer an evening appointment, but I can come at the other times indicated.

_____ Evening is the only time I can come.

_____   _____
Child's Name   **Parent's Signature**

CONFERENCE CONFIRMATION

The following time has been reserved for your conference. Please contact Hillside Preschool at 123-4567 if you will be unable to attend at this time. Thank you.

_____   _____
Child's name   Teacher's name

_____   _____
Conference time   Conference date

– –

CONFERENCE CONFIRMATION

The following time has been reserved for your conference. Please contact Hillside Preschool at 123-4567 if you will be unable to attend at this time. Thank you.

_____   _____
Child's name   Teacher's name

_____   _____
Conference time   Conference date

– –

CONFERENCE CONFIRMATION

The following time has been reserved for your conference. Please contact Hillside Preschool at 123-4567 if you will be unable to attend at this time. Thank you.

_____   _____
Child's name   Teacher's name

_____   _____
Conference time   Conference date

– –

CONFERENCE CONFIRMATION

The following time has been reserved for your conference. Please contact Hillside Preschool at 123-4567 if you will be unable to attend at this time. Thank you.

_____   _____
Child's name   Teacher's name

_____   _____
Conference time   Conference date

– –

ALL ABOUT ME
My Skills Record: _____ *School Year*

My name is _____

My age is _____ My birthdate is _____

My address is _____ My phone number is _____

My parents are _____

I can	I need help	
_____	_____	buttoning, snapping, and zipping my clothes
_____	_____	going to the toilet by myself
_____	_____	listening to others when it is their turn to talk
_____	_____	telling what I want or need
_____	_____	following simple directions
_____	_____	attending to a task
_____	_____	helping with pick up and clean up
_____	_____	playing with other children
_____	_____	taking turns and sharing
_____	_____	speaking in sentences of five or more words
_____	_____	telling a story
_____	_____	matching colors
_____	_____	identifying red, yellow, green, and blue
_____	_____	reciting rhymes, singing songs
_____	_____	telling how things are alike and different
_____	_____	identifying a circle, square, triangle
_____	_____	counting from one to ten
_____	_____	recognizing my first and last name when it is printed
_____	_____	printing my first name correctly
_____	_____	identifying a few letters of the alphabet
_____	_____	throwing and catching a ball
_____	_____	riding a tricycle
_____	_____	running, hopping, jumping, and skipping
_____	_____	using crayons with control
_____	_____	using scissors with control
_____	_____	working a puzzle of six or more pieces

My favorite activity is _____

_____

The children I play with most are _____

_____

Adapted from *Preschool Curriculum* by Dorothy Cunningham.

© 1990 by The Center for Applied Research in Education, Inc.

KINDERGARTEN ENTRANCE SKILLS

Child's name _____

Child's age _____ Date _____

SOCIAL SKILLS AND BEHAVIORS

_____ 1. Child communicates ideas and feelings to adults.

_____ 2. Child communicates ideas and feelings to other children.

_____ 3. Child plays in cooperative manner with other children.

_____ 4. Child shares toys and materials during play time.

_____ 5. Child shares toys and materials during structured activities.

_____ 6. Child puts away toys he or she played with.

_____ 7. Child puts away toys he or she did not play with when asked.

_____ 8. Child asks questions when he or she wants to know more, or doesn't understand what is being said.

_____ 9. Child speaks in four to six word sentences that are intelligible.

SCHOOL SKILLS AND BEHAVIORS

_____ 1. Child is able to walk in line for various activities.

_____ 2. Child hangs up coat and extra clothing.

_____ 3. Child waits his or her turn to speak in a group.

_____ 4. Child sits down in a group of children and listens.

_____ 5. Child obeys basic group rules.

_____ 6. Child follows one and two part directions.

_____ 7. Child finishes projects, assignments, tasks.

_____ 8. Child makes smooth transitions from one activity to another.

COGNITIVE SKILLS

_____ 1. Child is familiar with days of the week, months, holidays, and weather.

_____ 2. Child uses books appropriately—carries them, turns pages, returns them to preschool.

_____ 3. Child knows first and last name.

_____ 4. Child knows and sings several children's songs.

_____ 5. Child says color names for red, blue, green, yellow, and orange.

_____ 6. Child can name body parts.

_____ 7. Child counts and knows meaning of numbers.

_____ 8. Child matches like letters, designs, numbers.

_____ 9. Child is familiar with letters, but does not necessarily know them by sight or memory.

FORM 4-5

SELF-HELP SKILLS

_____ 1. Child uses appropriate table manners, such as sitting in seat, passing food, and using silverware.

_____ 2. Child eats within a reasonable amount of time.

_____ 3. Child puts on and takes off coat, boots, hat, and mittens.

_____ 4. Child uses tissue when needed and throws it away.

_____ 5. Child asks to use bathroom when necessary, and needs little or no help.

_____ 6. Child washes hands without help after toileting.

MOTOR SKILLS

_____ 1. Child uses materials like glue, paste, tape, stapler, scissors, markers, and crayons appropriately.

_____ 2. Child can use zippers and buttons.

_____ 3. Child can work puzzles of six or more pieces.

_____ 4. Child can throw, catch, and kick a ball.

_____ 5. Child can run, jump, hop, and walk a balance beam.

_____ 6. Child can ride a tricycle.

COMMENTS

_____

_____

_____

_____

_____

_____

_____

_____

_____

_____

_____

_____
Signature/Position

INDIVIDUALIZED PLAN FOR CHILD WITH SPECIAL NEEDS

Child's name _____

Planning for period beginning _____ and ending _____

To be evaluated on _____

Evaluation team _____

_____

_____

Goal for Child _____

_____

_____

_____

Plan for achieving goal _____

_____

_____

_____

_____

_____

Method of Evaluation _____

_____

_____

_____

_____

_____

Results of Evaluation _____

_____

_____

_____

_____

_____

_____

_____

Planning by   Evaluation by

_____   _____
Signature/Date   **Signature/Date**

_____   _____
Signature/Date   **Signature/Date**

_____   _____
Signature/Date   **Signature/Date**

DOCUMENTATION OF CONCERN FOR A CHILD

Date _____

Child's name _____

Nature of concern _____

_____

Detailed observation _____

_____

_____

_____

_____

_____

_____

_____

_____

_____

_____

_____

_____

_____

_____

What action will be taken? _____

_____

_____

_____

_____

_____

_____

_____

_____

_____

_____

_____

_____

Signature/Position

CHILD CONCERN LETTER

Date _____

Dear Parents,

      We, the staff at Hillside Preschool, are concerned about the growth and development of each of the children in our care. We have a concern about your child that we would like to make you aware of.

Child's name _____ Class _____

Concern _____

Explanation _____

_____

_____

_____

We would like your permission to take the following action:

    _____ Parent/teacher conference

    _____ Observation by behavior specialist

    _____ Evaluation by hearing specialist

    _____ Evaluation by vision specialist

    _____ Evaluation by speech therapist

    _____ Observation by learning disabilities specialist

    _____ Evaluation by school nurse/doctor

    _____ Other _____

We would like to discuss this matter further with you. We have set aside the following time to meet with you. If this is not convenient, please call me at 123–4567 during preschool hours.

Date _____   Time _____

_____
Signature/Position

PERMISSION FOR FURTHER EVALUATION

Date _____

Child's name _____

Concern _____

Explanation _____

_____

_____

_____

Recommended action _____

_____

_____

I feel this action is in the best interest of the above-named child. I give my permission for it to be carried out, with the understanding that I will be given a full report of the results.

_____   _____
Teacher/Position   **Parent/Date**

- -

PERMISSION FOR FURTHER EVALUATION

Date _____

Child's name _____

Concern _____

Explanation _____

_____

_____

_____

Recommended action _____

_____

_____

I feel this action is in the best interest of the above-named child. I give my permission for it to be carried out, with the understanding that I will be given a full report of the results.

_____   _____
Teacher/Position   **Parent/Date**

_____

HAS DONE A

TERRIFFIC
JOB

_____

RECORD OF CONFERENCES

Child's name _____

Parent's name _____

Staff Conducting Conference	Date	Parents Attend? Yes*	No

*Indicate father (f), mother (m), or both (b).

- -

RECORD OF CONFERENCES

Child's name _____

Parent's name _____

Staff Conducting Conference	Date	Parents Attend? Yes*	No

*Indicate father (f), mother (m), or both (b).

SECTION 5
CURRICULUM PLANNING

The forms in this section are meant to help you get your thoughts together concerning curriculum plans. They begin with an overview of the year, and become more specific until you have very detailed plans written for each period of each day. Again, color-coding the forms will help to organize all of these planning sheets.

5–1 Areas to Consider When Planning Curriculum is a sample list of curriculum and developmental concepts to keep in mind when planning curriculum for the preschool year. Design your list to include the areas of focus in your program.

5–2 Program Goals is a form for listing short- and long-range goals. It is designed to help you put future plans into focus.

5–3 Program Planning takes the general program goals from *Program Goals* and develops objectives, evaluation, and a time frame.

5–4 Curriculum Development works through the same type of goal development, but with very specific curriculum-related goals, which can lead directly into planning weekly activities.

5–5 Sample Director's Calendar is intended to remind you of all of those deadlines long before they come due. When you finish with your appointment calendar at the end of the year, add all of those important deadlines you met into your next year's *Director's Calendar* so you will be aware of them well in advance.

5–6 Yearly Planner is the place to record all of the unit topics that you intend to use for the entire school year.

5–7 Monthly Calendar is simply a manageable piece of the yearly planner; on it you can record units, special events, birthdays, and whatever else is important to you and to your class.

5–8 Unit Worksheet is a tool for brainstorming about all of the exciting things you could possibly do with one particular unit topic. Then you may take only the ideas you like the most and transfer them to a *Unit Calendar* or *Daily Planning Sheets*.

5–9 Unit Calendar is another calendar for the month, but is intended to record only those specific activities you choose to develop within curriculum areas. Each week or unit topic has its own row of cells in which to record those activities, thereby giving you an overview of the month at a glance.

5–10 Daily Planning Sheet records the activities you plan for each day within each of your curriculum areas. This is the "lesson plan" that should travel to class with you each day.

5–11 Daily Schedule is a chart that allows you to record the schedule you follow each day. The sample given here is for an all day program.

5–12 Parent Newsletter is the form to be sent to parents on a weekly basis to inform them of your planned curriculum and activities for the coming week.

AREAS TO CONSIDER WHEN PLANNING CURRICULUM

Curriculum Areas

Prereading/reading readiness
Math/numbers
Science/nature
Writing skills
Language development

Community
Field trips
Social skills
Self-help skills
Physical skills

Developmental Areas

Emotional:
    Self-awareness
    Self-concept
    Sense of family
    Self-care
    Self-responsibility

Self-control
Attention span
Completing a task
Smooth transitions
Delayed gratification

Social:
    Parallel play
    Cooperative play
    Dramatic play
    Role playing
    Communication with adults/peers
    Listening to adults/peers

Cleanliness/health/safety
Sense of community
Cultural awareness
Responsible use of materials
Etiquette
Sharing/taking turns

Physical:
    Body awareness
    Gross motor coordination
    Fine motor coordination

Eye-hand coordination
Eye-foot coordination

Senses:
    Music appreciation
    Visual memory
    Auditory memory
    Color discrimination

Music involvement
Creative expression
Tasting and smelling
Tactile awareness

Cognitive:
    Nature appreciation
    Numbers concepts
    Spacial concepts
    Conception of time

Visual discrimination
Auditory discrimination
Language development
Following directions

PROGRAM GOALS

Planner _____ Date _____

SHORT-RANGE GOALS

This month
    by _____
          (Date)

This quarter
    by _____
          (Date)

This semester
    by _____
          (Date)

This year
    by _____
          (Date)

LONG-RANGE GOALS

In one year
    by _____
          (Date)

In two years
    by _____
          (Date)

In five years
    by _____
          (Date)

In ten years
    by _____
          (Date)

PROGRAM PLANNING

Planning for period beginning _____ and ending _____

To be evaluated on _____

PROGRAM GOAL _____

_____

Objectives _____

_____

_____

Method of Evaluation _____

_____

_____

Results of Evaluation _____

_____

_____

PROGRAM GOAL _____

_____

Objectives _____

_____

_____

Method of Evaluation _____

_____

_____

Results of Evaluation _____

_____

_____

_____

_____

_____

_____

_____

_____

_____

_____

Planning by   Evaluation by

_____   _____
Signature/Date   Signature/Date

_____   _____
Signature/Date   Signature/Date

CURRICULUM DEVELOPMENT

Class_____ Teacher _____

Curriculum Area _____

Specific Goal _____
_____

   Steps to take in developing this goal _____
_____
_____

   Method of Evaluation _____
_____
_____

   Results of Evaluation _____
_____
_____

Specific Goal _____
_____

   Steps to take in developing this goal _____
_____
_____

   Method of Evaluation _____
_____
_____

   Results of Evaluation _____
_____
_____
_____
_____
_____
_____
_____
_____
_____
_____

Planning by   Evaluation by

_____   _____
Signature/Date   Signature/Date

_____   _____
Signature/Date   Signature/Date

SAMPLE DIRECTOR'S CALENDAR

JULY

1. Contact staff members to be sure each will be returning.
2. With Board, hire new staff, if necessary.
3. Submit preschool description to newspaper for inclusion in school news.

AUGUST

1. Revise registration materials and have them printed.
2. Order immunization forms from licensing agency.
3. Contact licensing agency; set up appointment for licensing consultation.
4. Check storeroom and kitchen for materials and supplies; restock materials and supplies as needed.
5. Compile a list of enrolled children from the latest registration information.
6. Referring to public school calendar, draw up preschool calendar for the coming year.
7. With Board, plan registration meeting for the Monday of the week before school starts.
8. Contact church to make arrangements for use of the facilities for the coming year, and for the registration meeting.
9. Have all materials printed and ready to hand out at registration.
10. Contact staff to be sure they will all attend the registration meeting.
11. Write registration letter and mail it to all parents by August 15.
12. Conduct registration meeting.

SEPTEMBER

1. After registration meeting, contact any parents who did not attend to see if they still plan to send their child.
2. Update the list of children and establish classes, giving copies of the class checklists to staff, Board President, and Treasurer.
3. Prepare a file for each child containing all registration materials.
4. Prepare a file for each staff member containing *Application for Employment,* Health Statement, and forms from each of three references.
5. Write first newsletter giving parents any additional information.
6. Ensure that fire drills will be conducted monthly.

OCTOBER

1. Immunization report form due at state office by October 15.
2. Coordinate planning of Halloween parties.

NOVEMBER

1. Begin plans for Holiday Party, make arrangements for the use of the church.
2. Coordinate parent conferences for each child, using one preschool day per class.

DECEMBER

1. Complete plans for Holiday Party.
2. Print programs for party.
3. Host Holiday Party.

JANUARY

1. Be prepared for annual visits by the state fire inspector and the state health inspector.
2. If there are any violations, report the correction of said violations in writing to appropriate agency.
3. File immunization report form with state office by January 15.
4. Begin plans for "The Week of the Young Child" in April, in conjunction with Early Childhood Association.

FEBRUARY

1. Prepare preregistration forms for coming year.
2. Begin preparing a budget proposal for the coming year.
3. Coordinate planning for Valentine parties.

MARCH

1. Send registration letter home with currently enrolled children, giving them the opportunity to preregister for the coming year.
2. Begin planning for preregistration open house in April or May.
3. Finalize and present budget proposal for the coming year.

APRIL

1. Celebration of "The Week of the Young Child."
2. Coordinate parent conferences.

MAY

1. Hold preregistration open house.
2. Finalize class and budget plans for coming year.
3. Plan end-of-year skating party for all children and their families.

YEARLY PLANNER

September
- Week 1 _____
- Week 2 _____
- Week 3 _____
- Week 4 _____
- Week 5 _____

October
- Week 1 _____
- Week 2 _____
- Week 3 _____
- Week 4 _____
- Week 5 _____

November
- Week 1 _____
- Week 2 _____
- Week 3 _____
- Week 4 _____
- Week 5 _____

December
- Week 1 _____
- Week 2 _____
- Week 3 _____
- Week 4 _____
- Week 5 _____

January
- Week 1 _____
- Week 2 _____
- Week 3 _____
- Week 4 _____
- Week 5 _____

February
- Week 1 _____
- Week 2 _____
- Week 3 _____
- Week 4 _____
- Week 5 _____

March

Week 1 _____

Week 2 _____

Week 3 _____

Week 4 _____

Week 5 _____

April

Week 1 _____

Week 2 _____

Week 3 _____

Week 4 _____

Week 5 _____

May

Week 1 _____

Week 2 _____

Week 3 _____

Week 4 _____

Week 5 _____

June

Week 1 _____

Week 2 _____

Week 3 _____

Week 4 _____

Week 5 _____

July

Week 1 _____

Week 2 _____

Week 3 _____

Week 4 _____

Week 5 _____

August

Week 1 _____

Week 2 _____

Week 3 _____

Week 4 _____

Week 5 _____

MONTHLY CALENDAR

Class _____

Month and Year _____

Sunday	Monday	Tuesday	Wednesday	Thursday	Friday	Saturday

FORM 5-7

UNIT WORKSHEET

Topic _____   Date used _____

Goals _____   Concepts _____

_____   _____

_____   _____

_____   _____

Vocabulary _____   Conversation time _____

_____   _____

_____   _____

_____   _____

Dramatic play _____   Small groups _____

_____   _____

_____   _____

_____   _____

Physical activities _____   Science _____

_____   _____

_____   _____

_____   _____

Outside resources/field trips _____   Creative activities _____

_____   _____

_____   _____

_____   _____

Songs and fingerplays _____   Cooking/snacks _____

_____   _____

_____   _____

_____   _____

Bulletin boards _____   Books _____

_____   _____

_____   _____

_____   _____

Special equipment, materials needed _____   Evaluation _____

_____   _____

_____   _____

_____   _____

UNIT CALENDAR

Month and Year _____

Class _____

Date	Unit	Science	Games	Field Trip	Art	Food	Songs

FORM 5-9

DAILY PLANNING SHEET

Unit topic _____   Date _____

Group Time _____
    Attendance _____
    Conversation _____
    Fingerplays _____
    Songs _____

Activity or Game _____

Story _____

Snack _____

Quiet Room _____
    Art _____
    Cognitive _____
    Music _____
    Science _____
    Books _____
    Other _____

Active Room _____
    Housekeeping _____
    Dramatic play _____
    Blocks _____
    Manipulatives _____
    Large muscle _____

DAILY SCHEDULE

Class _____

7:00–7:30 _____

   7:30–8:00 _____

8:00–8:30 _____

   8:30–9:00 _____

9:00–9:30 _____

   9:30–10:00 _____

10:00–10:30 _____

   10:30–11:00 _____

11:00–11:30 _____

   11:30–12:00 _____

12:00–12:30 _____

   12:30–1:00 _____

1:00–1:30 _____

   1:30–2:00 _____

2:00–2:30 _____

   2:30–3:00 _____

3:00–3:30 _____

   3:30–4:00 _____

4:00–4:30 _____

   4:30–5:00 _____

5:00–5:30 _____

   5:30–6:00 _____

FORM 5-11

PARENT NEWSLETTER

Date _____ Class _____

Teachers _____

Plans for the week of _____

Our unit topic will be _____

Special activities will include _____
_____
_____

Field trip _____

Special guest _____

Special foods will be _____
_____

Things to talk about at home _____
_____

Ways that you could help at preschool _____
_____

Special thanks to _____
_____

Looking forward to _____
_____

Reminders _____
_____

SECTION 6

FORMS FOR FIELD TRIPS

Although there was a general permission form in Section 3 allowing the child to go on field trips with the preschool, the forms in this section are specific to individual field trips. They also include methods of tracking which groups or individuals are out of the center, where they have gone, and when they will return.

6–1 Sample Request for Field Trip is an example of a letter requesting permission to bring a group of children for a field trip. It should be very specific about the ages of the children, the number of children and accompanying adults, what you would like the children to see, and how long you would like to be there. You should request permission about two weeks before you would like to visit. Include a specific date when you will call to see if permission will be granted, and to make any further necessary arrangements.

6–2 Sample Thank You for Field Trip is an example of a letter expressing appreciation for hosting a group of children. It is appropriate to include something very specific that made an impression on the children, and a description of how the experience fits into what they are learning at preschool.

6–3 Permission for Individual Field Trip informs the parents about individual field trips, and asks permission for the child to participate in the trip.

6–4 Individual Class Check-Out Form is to be completed for each class every time they leave the preschool building. The form is left with the secretary or in a central location where staff and/or parents can determine where a class is, and when it will return.

6–5 Class Check-Out Chart is for recording class check-out in a large center where several classes may be going different places at different times. The same information is contained in the *Individual Class Check-Out Form,* but the chart format allows quick reference when a number of classes are out.

6–6 Individual Child Check-Out Form is to be completed for each child every time he/she leaves the preschool building other than on a field trip with the class or home with the parent or designated pick-up person. The form is left with the secretary or in a central location where the staff and/or the parent can determine where a child is, and when he/she will return.

6–7 Child Check-Out Chart is for recording an individual child's check-out in a large center where several children leave to participate in different activities at different times. The same information is contained in the *Individual Child Check-Out Form,* but the chart format allows quick reference when a number of children are out.

6–8 Take-Along Emergency Information Form contains the names and phone numbers needed in case of an emergency away from the preschool building. It should be updated before each trip, and taken along whenever a class leaves the preschool building.

6–9 Permission for Special Outside Activity is to be completed by the parent and by the teacher, if appropriate, each time the child is to leave the preschool for an activity other than a field trip with the class, or home with a parent or designated pick-up person. Examples of such activities are swimming lessons during the summer or an appointment with an audiologist.

SAMPLE REQUEST FOR FIELD TRIP

(Your letterhead here)

March 17, 19 _____

King's Saddlery
348 North Scott
Anywhere, USA 56789

Dear Mr. King,

As director of Hillside Preschool I am writing to inquire if I may bring a group of children on a field trip to your place of business one morning during the week of March 21, 19 _____ . There will be 20 children 4–5 years of age, and 5 adults.

We will be talking about cowboys that week. Learning about how you make ropes and saddles will supplement the children's understanding of how a real cowboy lives and works.

Because the children are so young, a 15–20 minute tour would be appropriate. I would like them to see specifically what the rope is made of, how it is twisted, how long the ropes are, the many kinds and colors of ropes, which employees do what work, and examples of some of the saddles you have in stock.

I will call you Friday morning, March 11, to see if you would like to have us visit, and if so, when. If it would be more convenient, you may call me any day between 8:30 A.M. and 5:00 P.M. at 123-4567.

Cordially,

Rebecca Graff
Director

SAMPLE THANK YOU FOR FIELD TRIP

(Your letterhead here)

March 23, 19 _____

King's Saddlery
348 North Scott
Anywhere, USA 56789

Dear Mr. King,

    Thank you for welcoming the 4-year-old class of Hillside Preschool to your place of business. The children especially enjoyed seeing how Mr. Martin tied the knot in each end of the rope. They also have a better appreciation now for the art of roping, which is so essential for a cowboy.

                                                      Cordially,

                                                    Rebecca Graff
                                                    Director

PERMISSION FOR INDIVIDUAL FIELD TRIP

Hillside Preschool has a special field trip planned, and would like your permission to take your child. Please sign the lower half and send it back to preschool as soon as possible. Thank you.

Today's date _____   Date of Trip _____

Class going _____

We are going to _____

_____

Special considerations _____

_____

* *

Child's name _____

I give my permission for my child to go with Hillside Preschool staff to _____

_____ on _____

_____
Signature of Parent/Guardian

_____
Date

- -

PERMISSION FOR INDIVIDUAL FIELD TRIP

Hillside Preschool has a special field trip planned, and would like your permission to take your child. Please sign the lower half and send it back to preschool as soon as possible. Thank you.

Today's date _____   Date of Trip _____

Class going _____

We are going to _____

_____

Special considerations _____

_____

* *

Child's name _____

I give my permission for my child to go with Hillside Preschool staff to _____

_____ on _____

_____
Signature of Parent/Guardian

_____
Date

INDIVIDUAL CLASS CHECK-OUT FORM

Class _____

Date _____

Teachers _____

Going to _____

Method of travel _____

Number of children going _____

Number of adults going _____

Time out _____

Expected time in _____

— —

INDIVIDUAL CLASS CHECK-OUT FORM

Class _____

Date _____

Teachers _____

Going to _____

Method of travel _____

Number of children going _____

Number of adults going _____

Time out _____

Expected time in _____

CLASS CHECK-OUT CHART

Class	Date	Teacher Responsible	Going to	Travel Method	Number Children	Number Adults	Time Out	Time In	In

© 1990 by The Center for Applied Research in Education, Inc.

FORM 6-5

INDIVIDUAL CHILD CHECK-OUT FORM

Child _____ Date _____

Class _____

Going to _____

Method of travel _____ Parental permission on file _____

Today only, or regularly _____

Other children going _____

Who is accompanying child? _____

Time out _____ Expected time in _____

Authorized by _____

- -

INDIVIDUAL CHILD CHECK-OUT FORM

Child _____ Date _____

Class _____

Going to _____

Method of travel _____ Parental permission on file _____

Today only, or regularly _____

Other children going _____

Who is accompanying child? _____

Time out _____ Expected time in _____

Authorized by _____

CHILD CHECK-OUT CHART

Child	Date	Teacher Responsible	Going to	Travel Method	Others Going	Time Out	Time In	In

FORM 6-7

TAKE-ALONG EMERGENCY INFORMATION FORM

Child's Name Home Phone	Father's Name Work Phone	Mother's Name Work Phone	Physician Office Phone	Dentist Office Phone

PERMISSION FOR SPECIAL OUTSIDE ACTIVITY

Permission is required for your child to attend the following special activity outside of the normal program. Please sign the lower half of this form and send it back as soon as possible. Thank you.

Today's date _____

Date of special activity _____

Special activity _____

_____

Sponsored by _____

_____

Other children or adults attending _____

_____

Transportation arranged? _____

Special considerations _____

_____

_____

_____

_____

_____

* *

Child's name _____

I give my permission for my child to go to

_____

on this date _____

_____
Signature of Parent/Guardian

_____
Date

FORMS FOR
DAILY RECORD KEEPING

This section contains a number of forms which will help you plan and organize your daily record keeping. Three different staffing patterns are presented here. If one of these does not fit your needs exactly, it will, at least, get you started on some of the ways to plan staffing. Two different forms for keeping daily attendance are provided. The medical and health-related forms are meant to be supplemented by the forms your licensing agency supplies.

7–1 Staffing Pattern for Half-Day Program allows you to plan the class, room, teachers, and times when those things change depending upon the day of the week. A half-day preschool program that meets on Monday, Wednesday, and Friday mornings would use this type of staffing pattern.

7–2 Staffing Pattern for Full-Day Separate Classrooms is the type of pattern used by a day care center with a separate classroom for each age group. On this form, fill the squares with the name of the staff person who will be covering each classroom during each hour of the day.

7–3 Staffing Pattern for Full-Day Staffing by Position is best used by the program having the children together in one group for most of the day. The squares are filled with the activity or area each person will cover during each hour of the day.

7–4 Licensed Capacity is intended for a small program, such as a home day care with a number of different-aged children in the same group. This form is a method of accounting for how each child and staff person fits into the regulations for staff:child ratio.

7–5 Attendance Record is a chart to check off attendance each day.

7–6 Daily Time Sheet is designed for use in a small day care center where staff and children come and go at different times during the day. This sheet is especially useful for a program that charges fees by the hour. Parents should be expected to check the child in and out each day, so that comments may be written or read.

7–7 Sample Absent Child Follow-Up Letter is a letter to the parent of a child who has been absent without explanation. This letter is to be used after unsuccessful attempts to reach the parent by telephone.

7–8 Emergency Phone Numbers is a record of the phone numbers needed in an emergency. It is to be posted by each telephone in the preschool building, and updated as needed.

7–9 Emergency Drill Log is to be used for natural disasters, such as fire, tornado, or earthquake drills. These logs should be kept in a three-ring binder in the files.

7–10 Child's Preschool Record is to be kept in each child's file. On it can be recorded any incidents of note—problems, illnesses, exceptional progress—that are not already documented on a separate form. The same form can be used throughout the child's time in the program.

7–11 Schedule of Medications is an ongoing record of all of the children who are to be administered medications during preschool. It should be posted by or on the medicine cabinet. When the stop date is reached or the medication is gone, the child's name and record should be crossed off the form. The staff person who administers medications should be able to check the form daily to know which child gets which medication and when.

7–12 Individual Child's Record of Medications Given is a form started for the child each time a new medication is administered. The parent completes the top of the form when bringing the medication to preschool. The forms should be kept in a binder by the medicine cabinet and marked each time medication is administered. When the medication is gone or returned to the parent, the form should be filed in the child's record.

7–13 Accident Log is a running account of all of the accidents that happen during the preschool program, either on the premises or off. Each line in the log should correspond to an *Accident Report,* which should be kept in the same ring binder.

7–14 Accident Report is the form filled out for each accident that happens to a child or staff person while at preschool. It is to be completed within 24 hours of the accident, recorded on the *Accident Log,* and kept in the binder specifically for accidents. One copy of the report should go to the parent, and another copy placed in the child's file.

7–15 Child's Immunization Record must be completed and on file for each child before he/she is allowed to attend preschool. Updates are to be recorded as given.

STAFFING PATTERN FOR HALF-DAY PROGRAM

	Monday	Tuesday	Wednesday	Thursday	Friday
A.M. Class					
Teacher					
Teacher					
Age of Children					
Number of Children					
Room					

	Monday	Tuesday	Wednesday	Thursday	Friday
P.M. Class					
Teacher					
Teacher					
Age of Children					
Number of Children					
Room					

STAFFING PATTERN FOR FULL-DAY SEPARATE CLASSROOMS

	2-Year-Olds	3-Year-Olds	4-Year-Olds	5-Year-Olds	Kindergarten
A.M. 6–7					
7–8					
8–9					
9–10					
10–11					
11–12					
P.M. 12–1					
1–2					
2–3					
3–4					
4–5					
5–6					

STAFFING PATTERN FOR FULL-TIME STAFFING BY POSITION

	Director	Teacher	Teacher	Aide	Aide
A.M. 6–7					
7–8					
8–9					
9–10					
10–11					
11–12					
P.M. 12–1					
1–2					
2–3					
3–4					
4–5					
5–6					

LICENSED CAPACITY

Type of license _____ Date _____

	Licensed Number	Age	Name	Hours Each Day
Caregiver				
Infant				
Toddler				
Preschool				
School Age				

FORM 7-4

ATTENDANCE RECORD

Class _____

Month and year _____

Name	1	2	3	4	5	6	7	8	9	10	11	12	13	14	15	16	17	18	19	20	21	22	23	24	25	26	27	28	29	30	31
1																															
2																															
3																															
4																															
5																															
6																															
7																															
8																															
9																															
10																															
11																															
12																															
13																															
14																															
15																															
16																															
17																															
18																															
19																															
20																															

FORM 7-5

DAILY TIME SHEET

Date _____

Staff Name	Time In	Time Out	Comments

Child's Name	Time In	Time Out	Comments

FORM 7–6

SAMPLE ABSENT CHILD FOLLOW-UP LETTER

(Your letterhead here)

March 11, 19 _____

Dear Parents,

We missed Sarah in preschool on Friday and Monday, March 7 and 10. We were unable to contact you by phone, so are writing instead to inquire about the nature of your child's absence.

Has there been an illness? Has something happened at preschool? Is there a problem with which we can help? If so, please call anytime during preschool hours, 123-4567.

We certainly miss our children when they are absent from preschool. We hope to see Sarah in preschool again very soon.

Cordially,

Rebecca Graff
Director

EMERGENCY PHONE NUMBERS

TO BE POSTED BY PHONE

Fire department _____

Police department _____

Doctor or clinic on call _____

Dentist on call _____

Emergency transportation _____

Poison control center _____

Nearest hospital _____

Child protection team _____

Licensor _____

Emergency help or substitute _____

* *

This address is _____

_____

This phone number is _____

EMERGENCY PHONE NUMBERS

TO BE POSTED BY PHONE

Fire department _____

Police department _____

Doctor or clinic on call _____

Dentist on call _____

Emergency transportation _____

Poison control center _____

Nearest hospital _____

Child protection team _____

Licensor _____

Emergency help or substitute _____

* *

This address is _____

_____

This phone number is _____

EMERGENCY DRILL LOG

Year _____

Date	Elapsed Time	Comments	Person Responsible
September			
October			
November			
December			
January			
February			
March			
April			
May			
June			
July			
August			

FORM 7-9

CHILD'S PRESCHOOL RECORD

Name of student _____

Name of preschool _____

Date	Staff Filing Report	Comments
_____	_____	_____
_____	_____	_____
_____	_____	_____
_____	_____	_____
_____	_____	_____
_____	_____	_____
_____	_____	_____
_____	_____	_____
_____	_____	_____
_____	_____	_____
_____	_____	_____
_____	_____	_____
_____	_____	_____
_____	_____	_____
_____	_____	_____

FORM 7-10

SCHEDULE OF MEDICATIONS

TO BE POSTED NEAR MEDICINE CABINET

Date	Name	Medication	Dose	Times	Stop Date

FORM 7-11

INDIVIDUAL CHILD'S RECORD OF MEDICATIONS GIVEN

PARENT: COMPLETE TOP OF FORM AND BRING TO PRESCHOOL WITH MEDICATION.

Child's name _____

Medication _____

Dose/times _____

Administration of medication authorized by _____

Parent Signature/Date

* *

Date	Medication Given	Dose	Time	Given by

Medication _____ gone and container destroyed or _____ sent home with parent.

_____

Signature/Date

FORM 7-12

ACCIDENT LOG

Report Number	Date	Child Involved	Type of Accident	Action Taken

© 1990 by The Center for Applied Research in Education, Inc.

ACCIDENT REPORT

Report number _____

Child's name _____

Child's address _____

Age _____ Birthdate _____

Parents' names _____

Date of accident _____ Time of accident _____

Place of accident _____

Describe accident _____

_____

Describe nature of injury _____

_____

Witnessed by _____

What action was taken? _____

Taken to hospital? _____ Mode of transportation _____

By whom _____

Was parent contacted? _____ Other persons called _____

_____ Relationship _____

Was doctor called? _____

Follow-up _____

_____

Additional information _____

_____

_____

_____

_____

_____

_____

_____

_____

_____

_____

_____

_____

_____

_____

_____

_____   _____
Signature/Position   **Date**

FORM 7-14

CHILD'S IMMUNIZATION RECORD

Child's name _____

Enrollment date _____ Age at enrollment _____

Immunization	Date	Date	Date	Date	Date
DTP					
Td					
Polio					
M M R					
Measles					
Rubella					
Mumps					
Influenza					
TB Test					

Immunizations given by _____

Address _____

_____

Phone _____

Updated on (Circle years when updates are required, then fill in date as updates are done.)

6 months _____
1 year _____
2 years _____
3 years _____
4 years _____
5 years _____
6 years _____
7 years _____
8 years _____
9 years _____
10 years _____

FINANCIAL FORMS

The forms in this section fall into two major categories: forms having to do with tuition and the collection of fees, and forms for financial planning and monthly reporting. The tuition statements included here are examples of those used in different programs with different methods of assessing fees. Choose the one that best fits your needs, or use the ideas here to create your own unique billing system.

8–1 Provider's Contract is included as a basis for establishing a billing system with the parents in your program. This contract should be as specific as possible, especially with respect to financial arrangements and arrangements for vacations and sick time. Having an understanding at the start will help eliminate the embarrassment and frustration of misunderstandings at billing times. The original of this completed contract should go in the child's file, and a copy should go to the parent. If a third party is paying the tuition, that party should also receive a copy of the contract.

8–2 Scholarship Application can be used when scholarship money is available. Additional information can be requested depending on the eligibility requirements for your scholarship funds.

8–3 Tuition Statement (Paid per Session) is the statement used to bill for a number of sessions on a per-session basis.

8–4 Tuition Statement (Based on Hourly Fee) is the statement for billing on an hourly basis.

8–5 Tuition Statement (Flat Monthly Fee) is the statement used to bill when the fee is a flat rate per month, regardless of the number of sessions or hours.

8–6 Tuition Reminder is used in the program that bills a flat monthly fee. Print enough half-sheet reminders for the year with the current rate, preschool name, tuition collector, and finance charge. The reminders are then sent home with each of the children at the end of each month, thus saving the cost of envelopes and postage.

8–7 Sample Late Payment Letter notifies the parent that a child may not attend preschool unless past due bills are paid promptly. The payment schedule should be reasonable and individualized, preferably with the input of the parent.

8–8 *Income Worksheet* is used to help project income for the coming preschool year.

8–9 *Expenses Worksheet* enables you to project expenses for the coming year. If the worksheets are kept for past years and compared to actual year-end costs, those preparing the budget should be able to make fairly accurate projections for the coming year.

8–10 *Budget Projection* combines projected income and expenses to arrive at a predicted net gain or loss for the coming year.

8–11 *Monthly Financial Report* contains the same line items as the budget projections, but this form is for reporting actual income and expenses to date.

8–12 *Year-End Budget Analysis* requires the figures from the *Budget Projection* prepared at the beginning of the year with the "for year to date" figures from the final *Monthly Financial Report*. These projected and actual figures are compared per line item, gains or losses are computed, and adjustments are proposed for the next year's *Budget Projection*.

PROVIDER'S CONTRACT

Provider's name _____

    Provider's address _____

_____

Name(s) of child(ren) requiring care _____

_____

Father's name _____ Phone _____

    Father's address _____

    Father's occupation and place of employment _____

_____ Phone _____

Mother's name _____ Phone _____

    Mother's address _____

    Mother's occupation and place of employment _____

_____ Phone _____

Responsible person to call in emergency when parent cannot be reached

    Name _____ Phone _____

    Address _____

Persons authorized to pick up child _____

_____

_____

Persons who *may not* pick up child _____

_____

_____

FINANCIAL ARRANGEMENTS

Hours requiring care:

    Monday _____

    Tuesday _____

    Wednesday _____

    Thursday _____

    Friday _____

Fee rates

    Fee per month _____

    Fee per week _____

    Fee per day _____

    Fee per hour _____

Fees to be paid on _____ for the period of _____

Person responsible for payment of fees _____

     Address (if not parent listed above) _____

ARRANGEMENTS FOR VACATIONS AND SICK TIME

Provider's vacation _____

_____

If provider is ill _____

_____

Child's vacation _____

_____

If child is ill _____

_____

PROGRAM

Daily Schedule

    6:00 A.M. _____

    7:00 _____

    8:00 _____

    9:00 _____

  10:00 _____

  11:00 _____

  12:00 P.M. _____

    1:00 _____

    2:00 _____

    3:00 _____

    4:00 _____

    5:00 _____

    6:00 _____

Typical indoor activities _____

_____

_____

_____

Typical outdoor activities _____

_____

_____

_____

Typical outdoor activities _____

_____

Provisions for child with special needs _____

_____

_____

Field trips/transportation of children _____

_____

_____

Special activities outside of the daily program _____

_____

_____

Methods of discipline _____

_____

_____

Toileting _____

_____

_____

Napping _____

_____

_____

Meals and snacks _____

_____

_____

Clothing _____

_____

_____

Other arrangements _____

_____

_____

AGREEMENT

We have completed these policies together, and hereby agree upon their use for the child(ren)

_____

for the period beginning _____ and ending _____ .

_____   _____
Provider/Date   **Parent or Guardian/Date**

                                          _____
                                          Parent or Guardian/Date

FORM 8-1

SCHOLARSHIP APPLICATION

Funds are available from a private source to provide scholarships for children at Hillside Preschool. If you wish to be considered for a scholarship, please complete this application and submit it to the Director.

Child's name _____ Class _____

Parents' names (father) _____

(mother) _____

Child's birthdate _____ Date first enrolled at preschool _____

Is child living with _____ father _____ mother _____ both?

Ages and relationships of others in the household:

_____ _____

_____ _____

_____ _____

_____ _____

Total household income last month _____

Total projected income this month _____

Please list any unusual circumstances that would affect your child's eligibility for a scholarship.

_____

_____

_____

Do you wish a _____ total or _____ partial scholarship?

If partial, what percentage? _____

Application submitted by _____ Date _____

* *

Scholarship _____ granted or _____ denied

By action of _____

Comments _____

_____

_____

_____

_____

_____

_____

_____

_____ _____

Signature   **Date**

TUITION STATEMENT *(paid per session)*

Child's name _____

Billing period _____

Number of days (sessions) _____

Amount per day (session) _____

Amount due _____

Amount past due _____

Finance charge _____

Credit _____

Please pay this amount _____

Submit by the 5th of the month to _____

_____

_____

Thank you.

NOTE: Late payments are subject to a finance charge of:

_____

- -

TUITION STATEMENT *(paid per session)*

Child's name _____

Billing period _____

Number of days (sessions) _____

Amount per day (session) _____

Amount due _____

Amount past due _____

Finance charge _____

Credit _____

Please pay this amount _____

Submit by the 5th of the month to _____

_____

_____

Thank you.

NOTE: Late payments are subject to a finance charge of:

_____

TUITION STATEMENT *(based on hourly fee)*

Child's name _____

Billing period _____

Number of hours _____

Amount per hour _____

Amount due _____

Amount past due _____

Finance charge _____

Credit _____

Please pay this amount _____

Submit by the 5th of the month to _____

_____

_____

Thank you.

NOTE: Late payments are subject to a finance charge of:

_____

- -

TUITION STATEMENT *(based on hourly fee)*

Child's name _____

Billing period _____

Number of hours _____

Amount per hour _____

Amount due _____

Amount past due _____

Finance charge _____

Credit _____

Please pay this amount _____

Submit by the 5th of the month to _____

_____

_____

Thank you.

NOTE: Late payments are subject to a finance charge of:

_____

TUITION STATEMENT *(flat monthly fee)*

Child's name _____

Billing period _____

Rate per month _____

Amount due _____

Amount past due _____

Finance charge _____

Credit _____

Please pay this amount _____

Submit by the 5th of the month to _____

_____

_____

Thank you.

NOTE: Late payments are subject to a finance charge of:

_____

- -

TUITION STATEMENT *(flat monthly fee)*

Child's name _____

Billing period _____

Rate per month _____

Amount due _____

Amount past due _____

Finance charge _____

Credit _____

Please pay this amount _____

Submit by the 5th of the month to _____

_____

_____

Thank you.

NOTE: Late payments are subject to a finance charge of:

_____

TUITION REMINDER

Dear Parents,

This is a reminder that tuition is now due. Your check for $ _____ is to be made payable to _____ and mailed by the 5th of the month to:

_____

_____

_____

Thank you.

NOTE: Late payments are subject to a finance charge of

_____

TUITION REMINDER

Dear Parents,

This is a reminder that tuition is now due. Your check for $ _____ is to be made payable to _____ and mailed by the 5th of the month to:

_____

_____

_____

Thank you.

NOTE: Late payments are subject to a finance charge of

_____

SAMPLE LATE PAYMENT LETTER

(Your letterhead here)

Today's date

Mr. and Mrs. Parent
Street Address
Anywhere, USA 56789

Dear Parent,

It is with regret that I must inform you that, due to nonpayment of tuition, your child is no longer able to attend Hillside Preschool.

If you wish to reenter your child into preschool, past-due tuition in the amount of $ _____ must be paid according to the following payment schedule:

$ _____ in full by February 1

$ _____ in full by February 15

$ _____ in full by March 1

$ _____ in full by March 15

$ _____ in full by April 1

If you wish to discuss this matter, please call me at 123-4567 during school hours.

Sincerely,

Rebecca Graff
Director
Hillside Preschool

INCOME WORKSHEET

Year:	Per Month	Per Year
Tuition		
Other fees		
Grant monies		
Federal		
State		
County		
City		
Other		
Food program		
Private donations		
Other income		
Total		

EXPENSES WORKSHEET

Year:	Cost/Month	Cost/Year
Director's Salary		
Teachers' salaries		
Aides' salaries		
Substitute staffs' wages		
Custodian's salary		
Cook's salary		
Additional staffs' salaries		
Continuing education costs		
Payroll taxes and benefits		
Rent or mortgage payment		
Maintenance costs		
Utilities		
Telephone		
Transportation costs		
Legal fees		
Accounting and auditing fees		
Bank fees		
Insurance		
Advertising		
Administrative supplies		
Postage		
Classroom supplies		
Books and printed materials		
Equipment		
Food		
Food service		
Cleaning supplies		
Other expenses		
Total		

BUDGET PROJECTION

For period _____ through _____

	Per Month	Per Year
INCOME		
Tuition		
Other fees		
Grant money		
Food program		
Private donations		
Other income		
Total projected income		
EXPENSES		
Combined salaries/wages		
Taxes/benefits		
Continuing education		
Building costs		
All utilities		
Transportation costs		
Professional fees		
Insurance		
Advertising		
Administrative/postage		
Classroom supplies		
Equipment		
Food costs		
Other costs		
Total projected expenses		
NET GAIN/LOSS		

MONTHLY FINANCIAL REPORT

For period _____ through _____

	This Month	For Year to Date
INCOME		
Tuition		
Other fees		
Grant money		
Food program		
Private donations		
Other income		
Total income		
EXPENSES		
Combined salaries/wages		
Taxes/benefits		
Continuing education		
Building costs		
All utilities		
Transportation costs		
Professional fees		
Insurance		
Advertising		
Administrative/postage		
Classroom supplies		
Equipment		
Food costs		
Other costs		
Total expenses		

PREVIOUS BALANCE _____

MONTH'S INCOME _____

MONTH'S EXPENSES _____

CURRENT BALANCE _____

_____
Submitted by

_____
Position

© 1990 by The Center for Applied Research in Education, Inc.

YEAR-END BUDGET ANALYSIS

For period _____ through _____

	Projection	Actual	+ or −	Next Year
INCOME				
Tuition				
Other fees				
Grant money				
Food program				
Private donations				
Other income				
Total income				
EXPENSES				
Combined salaries/wages				
Taxes/benefits				
Continuing education				
Building costs				
All utilities				
Transportation costs				
Professional fees				
Insurance				
Advertising				
Administrative/postage				
Classroom supplies				
Equipment				
Food costs				
Other costs				
Total expenses				

BEGINNING BALANCE _____

YEAR'S INCOME   _____

YEAR'S EXPENSES   _____

ENDING BALANCE   _____

_____
Submitted by

_____
Position

YEAR-END BUDGET ANALYSIS

For period _____ through _____

	Projection	Actual	+ or −	Next Year
INCOME				
Tuition				
Other fees				
Grant money				
Food program				
Private donations				
Other income				
Total income				
EXPENSES				
Combined salaries/wages				
Taxes/benefits				
Continuing education				
Building costs				
All utilities				
Transportation costs				
Professional fees				
Insurance				
Advertising				
Administrative/postage				
Classroom supplies				
Equipment				
Food costs				
Other costs				
Total expenses				

BEGINNING BALANCE _____

YEAR'S INCOME   _____

YEAR'S EXPENSES   _____

ENDING BALANCE   _____

_____
Submitted by

_____
Position

© 1990 by The Center for Applied Research in Education, Inc.

FORM 8–12

ADVERTISING SAMPLES

This section offers samples of advertising in many forms so that you may take from each what is best for your program. This is one of the areas where you can become very creative in selling your program to the public.

9-1 Fund-Raising Letter is an appeal for funds to those who have supported your program in the past, as well as any prospective supporters you have encountered in the last year. Businesses and organizations that support programming for children are good possibilities for starting a new mailing list.

9-2 Publicity Flyer is printed on a half-sheet of brightly colored paper, then distributed in any number of ways: on car windshields in the shopping mall, in grocery bags at the neighborhood store, on the literature rack at the YMCA or YWCA, at the laundromat, or through the welcome hostess in your community.

9-3 Elements of a News Release lists some of the important points to remember when writing a news release.

9-4 Sample News Release covers the opening of a new preschool, which follows those points.

9-5 Newspaper Ads gives examples of classified ads that may be written for a number of different types of early childhood programs. Personalize yours and make it say something about you.

9-6 Business Card is an actual business card in use in a preschool. If you have a logo (see logo contest below), this would be a good means of making it known throughout your community. A professional business card makes a statement about the professionalism of your preschool.

9-7 T-Shirt Logo Contest explains the desire for a logo, and the rewards for the best entry. The announcement is sent home with each of the children enrolled in the program, as well as to those who are registered for the coming year.

9–8 T-Shirt Order Form announces the winner of the logo contest, at the same time allowing the parents the opportunity to order t-shirts for their children and families. By encouraging the children to wear preschool t-shirts each time you take a field trip, you make your group more easily identifiable and lessen the likelihood of losing a child in a crowd.

9–9 Recipe Book Letter is sent home with each of the children to announce a project in which all families can participate. It makes a nice keepsake for children and their parents to have a recipe collection from their preschool. It is also a relatively simple fund-raiser if you can get a bargain on paper and printing.

9–10 Recipe Book Order Form is the form sent home with each child when the recipe book is ready to order. With advance orders, you can print only the number of books you will need. This form then provides you with a record of who ordered how many books.

FUND-RAISING LETTER

VALLEY DAY CARE CENTER
1234 Elm Street
Anywhere, USA 56789
Today's Date

Dear Friends,

The week of November 11th–17th has been designated as Valley Day Care Center's annual fund drive week. As you know, this is the time when we appeal to you, our friends and supporters, to contribute generously to the continued operation of this service for the children of our community.

Valley Center provides supervised day care for infants through school-aged children. Among the services are: the infant program for normal and handicapped children from ages 2 months through 2 years; our preschool program, ages 2 through kindergarten age, which prepares a child for formal schooling; our latch-key program, which provides before- and after-school care for school-aged children; individualized programming for handicapped children; and family and behavioral program counseling.

Valley Center has a current enrollment of 110 children, with an average daily attendance of 90. The professional staff numbers 7, the child care staff numbers 20, giving an overall staff-child ratio of 1:4.

Valley Center depends entirely upon local private monies and parent fees for its operation. Your contribution will help provide the loving care and instruction so many children in our community have come to rely upon. Your tax-deductible contribution may be sent to:

Valley Day Care Center
1234 Elm Street
Anywhere, USA 56789

Our annual open house will be held on Sunday, November 11 from 2:00 to 4:00 P.M. Please come to meet our staff and see what your past contributions have done for Valley Center.

With many thanks from the Board of Directors, staff, and especially the children of Valley Day Care Center.

Board President   Fund Drive Chairperson

PUBLICITY FLYER

Looking for a summer-only program for your preschool-aged child? Then check the YMCA summer tabloid for

LITTLE EXPLORERS

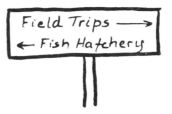

This group will meet three mornings a week at the Y. It will include fun and exploring in a warm, supportive atmosphere.

For more information and registration see the YMCA summer tabloid, to be out soon.

ELEMENTS OF A NEWS RELEASE

1. Type on 8½ × 11 nonerasable paper.

2. Leave wide margins and double space.

3. Limit to one page whenever possible—make it tight.

4. Name, address, and telephone number of author at upper left.

5. Release date, usually "Immediate Release," on right margin.

6. Do not write a headline, but leave space between the release line and body for editor to add headline.

7. Use the summary lead indicating who, what, where, when, why.

8. Use the code "###" to mark the end of your copy.

9. Make copy accurate, crisp, smooth; short direct sentences; active verbs.

10. Make it newsworthy, interesting; answer any questions reader might have.

11. Mail first class to each news organization, addressed to editor or news director (by name if possible).

SAMPLE NEWS RELEASE

Rebecca Graff, Director
Hillside Preschool
1234 Elm Street
Anywhere, USA 56789
Tel: (123) 456-7890

<u>Immediate Release</u>

Hillside Preschool, a new half-day learning experience for pre-school-aged children, is opening this fall. They will be hosting their open house/registration on Monday, August 1, from 6:30 to 8:30 P.M. at their location at 1234 Elm Street in Anywhere.

The public is invited to tour the new facility, meet the staff, and share refreshments. Children of all ages are welcome. Parents may register their children for classes, which begin September 2.

Hillside Preschool offers options for morning or afternoon sessions, for three to five days a week. Children who are three to six years of age on September 1 are welcome to enroll.

According to Director Rebecca Graff, the preschool will emphasize hands-on learning experiences. The children will take frequent field trips into the community. Food preparation, creative arts, working with tools, and computer experiences will be a major portion of the curriculum.

###

FORM 9-4

NEWSPAPER ADS

For a Preschool:

FUN & LEARNING! Hillside Preschool is now accepting registrations for 3- & 4-year-old half-day classes. For information, please call Director Rebecca Graff at 123-4567.

For a Day Care Center:

RELIABLE, CHILD-CENTERED CARE! Valley Day Care Center has openings for children 16 months through kindergarten age. 6 A.M. to 6 P.M., M-F. To visit, call Director Rebecca Graff at 123–4567.

For Latch Key:

AFTER-SCHOOL PROGRAM for school-agers K and up. Snacks, lots of activities. 3:00 to 6:30 P.M., M-F. Close to Lincoln School. Call Director Rebecca Graff at YWCA Latchkey at 123–4567.

For Infant Care:

INDIVIDUALIZED, LOVING in-center care for infants 1 month through 16 months. 6 A.M. to 6 P.M., M-F. Call Rebecca Graff at Hilltop Infant Center at 123–4567.

For Home Day Care:

WARM, LOVING home day care has 3 openings for toddler through school-age, 7 A.M. – 5:30 P.M., M-F. Close to Lincoln School. Call Rebecca Graff at 123–4567.

For Any Program:

LIST CONCISELY what kind of a program, a few words of description, ages, hours, number of openings if appropriate, who to contact, where, & how.

NOAH'S ARK
A CHRISTIAN PRESCHOOL

135 CRESCENT DRIVE
(TRINITY LUTHERAN CHURCH)
SHERIDAN, WYOMING

ANNOUNCING

T-SHIRT LOGO CONTEST

Design a T-Shirt and Win Shirts for Your Entire Family

Hillside Preschool wants to get in on the t-shirt craze, but what should we put on our shirts?

Calling all creative moms, dads, grandparents, and friends. This is your big chance to show us your talents. Draw your design ideas and submit them for judging by February 1. A committee from the Board and staff will select the most appropriate logo and announce the winner on Valentine's Day. At that time orders will be taken for t-shirts for all, and the talented winner of the contest will receive free shirts for the entire family.

So get out your paper and pencil, and draw a design that will convey the philosophy of our preschool. And good luck!

ANNOUNCING

T-SHIRT LOGO CONTEST

Design a T-Shirt and Win Shirts for Your Entire Family

Hillside Preschool wants to get in on the t-shirt craze, but what should we put on our shirts?

Calling all creative moms, dads, grandparents, and friends. This is your big chance to show us your talents. Draw your design ideas and submit them for judging by February 1. A committee from the Board and staff will select the most appropriate logo and announce the winner on Valentine's Day. At that time orders will be taken for t-shirts for all, and the talented winner of the contest will receive free shirts for the entire family.

So get out your paper and pencil, and draw a design that will convey the philosophy of our preschool. And good luck!

FORM 9-7

T-SHIRT ORDER FORM

ANNOUNCING

What:	HILLSIDE PRESCHOOL T-SHIRTS
Winner of logo contest:	The Sam Jacobs family
Cost:	$5.00 per shirt for children's sizes $6.50 per shirt for adults' sizes
Color:	Navy blue shirt with light blue logo
Logo:	Circle of children surrounding ABC blocks
To order:	Fill out the order form below and return it to preschool.
When:	Reserve your shirts NOW. Orders will be placed on February 21 for delivery by March 1.
Payment:	May be made now or upon delivery.
Thank you:	To each of the families who designed and entered a logo, your interest and support are great!

* *

Child's name _____

Size: child _____ S (2–4)   _____ M (6–8)   _____ L (10–12)   _____ XL (14–16)

      adult _____ S (34–36)   _____ M (38–40)   _____ L (42–44)   _____ XL (46)

© 1990 by The Center for Applied Research in Education, Inc.

RECIPE BOOK LETTER

(Your letterhead here)

January 3, 19 _____

Dear Parents,

We have begun working on an exciting fund-raising project and we need your help. We are compiling a recipe book that will contain recipes specifically geared to preschool-aged children. Planned sections are munchies, fruit and veggie snacks, cookies and bars, desserts, frozen treats, beverages, and holiday specialties. The last section will be "kid stuff"—things like playdough and rock gardens, which children can do for fun and discovery.

The Staff and Board are busy collecting their favorites, especially the recipes that children can make for themselves with very little help. Please check with your young person to see what his or her favorites are, and what he or she would like to share with other children, then send them to preschool. Our recipe book will be a wonderful, useful keepsake if each of the children adds a few recipes.

Thank you for your recipes and for your continuing support.

Hillside Preschool Staff and Board

RECIPE BOOK ORDER FORM

ANNOUNCING

What: HILLSIDE PRESCHOOL RECIPE BOOKS

Cost: $5.00 per book

Contains: Munchies, fruit and veggie snacks, cookies, desserts, frozen treats, beverages, holidays, and kid stuff

Description: Recipe card size to fit into your files
Color-coded sections

Gift ideas: Thoughtful gift for young mothers, children's parties

To order: Fill out the order form below and return it to preschool.

When: Reserve your recipe books NOW.
Orders will be placed on April 15 for delivery on May 1.

Payment: May be made now or upon delivery.

Thank you: To each of the families who contributed recipes, your interest and support are great!

* *

Child's name _____

Number of recipe books ordered _____

Amount, if payment is enclosed _____

© 1990 by The Center for Applied Research in Education, Inc.

FORM 9-10

SECTION 10
ADMINISTRATIVE FORMS

This section contains a potpourri of forms for keeping track of and ordering various kinds of supplies, as well as for managing the nuts and bolts necessary to keep any business orderly.

10–1 Memo is used to jot informal messages to staff, Board, or parents.

10–2 Messages can be printed on a whole sheet, and cut into six message forms. They can be used for taking messages by the phone and at the reception desk.

10–3 Infants' Equipment Inventory is a list of standard equipment necessary for an infant program. Additional equipment can be added on the blank lines. Inventory should be taken at the end of each year and replenished as needed.

10–4 Toddlers' Equipment Inventory is the same type of inventory but for a toddler program.

10–5 Preschool Equipment Inventory is for a preschool-age program.

10–6 School-Age Equipment Inventory is for a latchkey program.

10–7 Equipment Order Form is the follow-up to the inventory forms. Whatever equipment is lacking can be recorded on the order form and submitted for purchase.

10–8 Supplies Order Form is to be used any time during the year when supplies need to be replenished. It can be used as a shopping list.

10–9 Groceries Order Form is a shopping list for needed groceries, or it could also be used as an inventory list when that is needed.

10–10 Safety Equipment Maintenance Checklist is to be used during the semi-annual safety inspection. Each unit should be listed on a separate line. As that unit is inspected and found safe, it should be dated and initialed. As new equipment is added, be sure to add it to this checklist along with its installation date.

10–11 Requisition Form is the order form to be used for a supplier that does not provide its own order forms.

10–12 Reimbursement Form is to be submitted by any employee who spent his or her own money for preschool supplies, and wishes to be reimbursed. Receipts should be attached.

10–13 Lending Library Record is for tracking those books, puzzles, games, or equipment you lend to other professionals or to parents. The "returned" column requires only a checkmark for you to know that it has come back.

10–14 Service Request is the method of notification to whoever does your maintenance work that a job needs to be done. It would be best to walk that person through the location and describe the service required, if possible.

10–15 Director's Report is a quick reference form for putting together a monthly report for a Board or staff meeting. These reports should then be filed, along with minutes or notes and agenda from each meeting.

10–16 Parent Evaluation of Program is the final, end-of-year evaluation of all you have done as a preschool for the year coming to a close. It can be a wonderful learning tool for you and your staff to discover what parents feel you have been doing right, and what they feel needs improvement. It can be sent home with each child about a month before preschool is out, or mailed to each family if you prefer. Assuring parents that it will be anonymous may increase your chances of honest responses.

MEMO

Date:

To:

From:

Re:

MESSAGE

For _____
From _____
Of _____
Phone # _____
Date _____
Message _____
_____
_____

	called
	stopped in
	please call
	will call back
	taken by

MESSAGE

For _____
From _____
Of _____
Phone # _____
Date _____
Message _____
_____
_____

	called
	stopped in
	please call
	will call back
	taken by

MESSAGE

For _____
From _____
Of _____
Phone # _____
Date _____
Message _____
_____
_____

	called
	stopped in
	please call
	will call back
	taken by

MESSAGE

For _____
From _____
Of _____
Phone # _____
Date _____
Message _____
_____
_____

	called
	stopped in
	please call
	will call back
	taken by

MESSAGE

For _____
From _____
Of _____
Phone # _____
Date _____
Message _____
_____
_____

	called
	stopped in
	please call
	will call back
	taken by

MESSAGE

For _____
From _____
Of _____
Phone # _____
Date _____
Message _____
_____
_____

	called
	stopped in
	please call
	will call back
	taken by

INFANTS' EQUIPMENT INVENTORY

FURNITURE		MANIPULATIVES	
	cribs		nesting toys
	portable cribs		blocks
	highchairs		beads
	changing tables		stacking toys
	strollers		
	infant swings	COGNITIVE	
	infant seats		books
	johnny jump-up		busy boxes
	diaper pail		mobiles
	floor pillows		
	throw rugs or blankets	LARGE MUSCLE EQUIPMENT	
			balls
FOOD SERVICE			pull toys
	bottles		riding toys
	sterilizing equipment		large soft toys
	feeding spoons		large blocks
	baby food warmers		tunnels
			shapes
LINENS		SENSORY STIMULATION	
	waterproof mattress pads		shapes
	sheets		colors
	blankets		soft stuffed toys
	wash cloths		chew toys
	baby wipes		colorful dolls
	towels		mirrors
	diapers		
	bibs	NOISE MAKING	
			rattles
MUSIC			
	record player		
	tape player		
	music boxes		
	drums		

Submitted by _____   Date _____

TODDLERS' EQUIPMENT INVENTORY

FURNITURE		MANIPULATIVES	
	cribs		nesting toys
	cots		blocks
	beds		beads with strings
	mats		stacking toys
	highchairs		interlocking forms
	booster seats		shapes puzzle balls
	strollers		
	changing tables	COGNITIVE	
	diaper pail		books
	potty chair		busy boxes
	step stool		puzzles
	tables		puppets
	chairs		magnifying glass
	floor pillows		
	toy boxes	MUSIC	
	easels		record player
			tape player
FOOD SERVICE			music boxes
	cups		rhythm band instruments
	dishes		piano or keyboard
	silverware		
		SENSORY STIMULATION	
LINENS			shapes
	waterproof mattress pads		colors
	sheets		sand, water, or grain table
	blankets		playdough
	pillows		
	towels		
	washcloths		
	baby wipes		
	diapers		
	bibs		

FORM 10-4

LARGE MUSCLE EQUIPMENT	CREATIVE DRAMATIC PLAY
balls	dress-up clothes
pull and push toys	hats
riding toys	dolls and stuffed animals
large blocks	kitchen area
climber	transportation toys
rocking boat	tools
tunnel	mirrors
slide	telephone
swing	

Submitted by   **Date**

PRESCHOOL EQUIPMENT INVENTORY

FURNITURE		MANIPULATIVES	
	mats		peg boards
	cots		blocks
	beds		beads with strings
	booster seats		sewing cards
	strollers		interlocking forms
	potty chair		shapes puzzle balls
	step stool		
	tables		
	chairs		
	floor pillows		
	toy boxes and shelves		
	easels	COGNITIVE	
			books
			flannel board
			puzzles
			puppets
FOOD SERVICE			play towns
	cups		board games
	dishes		card games
	silverware		
LINENS			
	sheets	MUSIC	
	blankets		record player
	pillows		tape player
	towels		music boxes
	washclothes		rhythm band instruments
			piano or keyboard

FORM 10-5

LARGE MUSCLE EQUIPMENT		SENSORY STIMULATION	
	sports equipment		shapes
	riding toys		colors
	large transportation toys		sand, water, or grain table
	large blocks		playdough
	climber		sandpaper letters and numbers
	balance beam		
	rocking boat		
	tunnel		
	slide		
	swing		
	jump ropes	CREATIVE DRAMATIC PLAY	
	bean bags		dress-up clothes
			hats
			dolls and stuffed animals
			kitchen area
SCIENCE AND MATH MATERIALS			transportation toys
	magnifying glass		tools
	globe		mirrors
	magnets		telephones
	solid geometric shapes		
	computer		

Submitted by   **Date**

© 1990 by The Center for Applied Research in Education, Inc.

SCHOOL-AGE EQUIPMENT INVENTORY

FURNITURE		MANIPULATIVES	
	tables		Lincoln logs
	chairs		legos
	floor pillows		tinker toys
	toy boxes and shelves		hammer and nails
	easels		screwdriver and screws
			wrench and nuts
			saw and boards
FOOD SERVICE			
	cups		
	dishes	**COGNITIVE**	
	silverware		books
			puzzles
			flannel board
LARGE MUSCLE EQUIPMENT			puppets
	baseballs, bats, and gloves		play towns
	soccer balls		board games
	footballs		card games
	basketballs		
	volleyballs		
	soft playballs		
	outdoor climber		
	outdoor swings	**MUSIC**	
	outdoor sandbox		record player
	balance beam		tape player
	jump ropes		music boxes
	bean bags		rhythm band instruments
	wooden blocks and boards		piano or keyboard
	stilts		

SCIENCE AND MATH MATERIALS	SENSORY STIMULATION
live small pets	feelie bag
magnifying glass	smelling jars
prism	sand, water, or grain table
microscope	playdough
magnets	sandpaper letters and numbers
skeleton	
globe	
maps	
solid geometric shapes	CREATIVE DRAMATIC PLAY
abacus	occupation props
rulers	hats and uniforms
number games	dolls with clothes
calculator	kitchen area
computer	office area
	transportation toys
	puppet stage
	mock-TV

Submitted by _____   **Date** _____

EQUIPMENT ORDER FORM

Puzzles _____

_____

_____

_____

Books _____

_____

_____

_____

Records _____

_____

_____

_____

Tapes _____

_____

_____

Musical _____

_____

_____

Language arts _____

_____

_____

Holiday items _____

_____

_____

Science materials _____

_____

_____

_____

Math materials _____

_____

_____

_____

Manipulatives _____

_____

_____

_____

Small equipment _____

_____

_____

Large equipment _____

_____

_____

Dramatic play _____

_____

_____

Other _____

_____

_____

Submitted by _____   **Date** _____

FORM 10-7

SUPPLIES ORDER FORM

ART SUPPLIES			
	crayons		poster paints
	multicolor		red
	single color		yellow
	water color sets		blue
	replacements		green
	tempera powder		white
	red		black
	yellow		construction paper
	blue		red
	green		yellow
	white		blue
	black		green
	finger paint		white
	powder		black
	premixed		tag board
	red		red
	yellow		yellow
	blue		blue
	green		green
	white		white
	black		black
	pencils		easel paper
	markers		finger paint paper
	multicolor		other paper
	single color		
	paint brushes	CRAFT SUPPLIES	
	scissors		cotton balls
	glue		glitter
	paste		toothpicks
	tape		stickers
	masking		yarn
	transparent		
	colored		

PAPER PRODUCTS		ADMINISTRATIVE SUPPLIES	
	tissues		paper
	toilet tissue		staples
	paper towels		copies
	napkins		copy fluid/toner
	garbage bags		pens
	food bags		stamps
CLEANING SUPPLIES		**FOOD ITEMS**	
	cleanser		milk
	toilet bowl cleaner		juice
	disinfectant		punch
	dish detergent		crackers
	hand soap		fruit
			snacks
HOLIDAY ITEMS			

Submitted by _____   Date _____

GROCERIES ORDER FORM

STAPLES		FROZEN	
	flour		meat
	sugar		fish
	baking soda		fruits
	baking powder		vegetables
	corn starch		fruit juice
	powdered milk		drinks
	cocoa		desserts
	vanilla		
	shortening	MEATS	
	salad oil		fish
	rice		pork
	pasta		lamb
	beans		beef
	cereals		luncheon meats
	baking mixes		other meats
SPICES		FRESH PRODUCE	
	salt		potatoes
	seasoned salt		onions
	pepper		carrots
	cinnamon		celery
	chile powder		lettuce
			tomatoes
CONDIMENTS			bananas
	jelly		oranges
	peanut butter		apples
	honey		other fruits
	syrup		other vegetables
	ketchup		
	mustard		
	salad dressing		
	pickles		
	sauces		

CANNED GOODS		DAIRY	
	vegetables		milk
	fruits		butter
	fruit/vegetable juices		margarine
	soups		cream
	meat		cheese
	fish		cottage cheese
			eggs
SNACKS			yogurt
	crackers		
	cookies	BAKERY	
	popcorn		bread
	chips		buns
	nuts		rolls
	seeds		pastry
	gelatin		biscuits
	pudding		
	marshmallows	PAPER PRODUCTS	
			paper plates
MISCELLANEOUS			paper cups
	handsoap		paper napkins
	dish detergent		paper towels
	band aids		waxed paper
	first aid cream		aluminum foil
			facial tissues
			toilet tissue
			food storage bags
			garbage bags

(Submitted by) _____   **(Date)** _____

SAFETY EQUIPMENT MAINTENANCE CHECKLIST

Instal-lation Date	List Each Unit	Date and Checked by				
	Furnace					
	Fireplace/woodburner					
	Fire alarm					
	Emergency lighting					
	Smoke detectors					
	Fire extinguishers					
	First aid kit					

FORM 10-10

REQUISITION FORM

Vender

_____

_____

_____

_____

Send to

_____

_____

_____

_____

Quant.	Size	Order Number	Name	Price	Total
				Tax	
				Shipping	
				Total	

_____
(Authorized Signature)

_____ Payment enclosed

_____ Bill

Send via _____ UPS

_____ postal service

_____ best way

Bill to _____

_____

_____

_____

_____

_____

FORM 10-11

REIMBURSEMENT FORM

Employee name _____

Date _____

Date	Purchase	From	Amount

Please attach all receipts.

_____   _____
Employee Signature/Date   **Supervisor Signature/Date**

* *

The following is approved for reimbursement _____

_____
Authorized Signature/Date

LENDING LIBRARY RECORD

Name of Book/Material	Borrower	Phone Number	Date	Re-turned

SERVICE REQUEST

Date _____

Location requiring service _____

Description of service required _____

_____

_____

Date service should be completed _____

_____   _____
Requesting Signature   **Authorizing Signature**

- -

SERVICE REQUEST

Date _____

Location requiring service _____

Description of service required _____

_____

_____

Date service should be completed _____

_____   _____
Requesting Signature   **Authorizing Signature**

FORM 10-14

DIRECTOR'S REPORT

Date of report _____ For period of _____

Reported to _____

Submitted by _____

Current enrollment _____
    Children dropped _____
    Children added _____

Registrations for future enrollment _____

Financial report _____
_____
_____

Staff concerns _____
_____

Program concerns _____
_____

Special activities _____
_____

Old business _____
_____

New business _____
_____

Other _____
_____
_____

PARENT EVALUATION OF PROGRAM

The staff tries to provide the best preschool experience possible for your child. You can help us evaluate how we are doing by completing this form and returning it to your child's teacher as soon as possible. Please feel free to make comments. You do not need to sign your name, unless you would like a personal response to your concerns.

Please rate each item on a scale of 1-10, with 10 being "the best" and 1 being "the worst." Circle your choice. Consider primarily your child's reaction to the program, and then yours.

Thank you for your input, and for your support throughout the year.

Your child's class _____

PROGRAM CONTENT

Curriculum

| 10 | 9 | 8 | 7 | 6 | 5 | 4 | 3 | 2 | 1 |

Age appropriate

| 10 | 9 | 8 | 7 | 6 | 5 | 4 | 3 | 2 | 1 |

Academics

| 10 | 9 | 8 | 7 | 6 | 5 | 4 | 3 | 2 | 1 |

Creative outlets

| 10 | 9 | 8 | 7 | 6 | 5 | 4 | 3 | 2 | 1 |

Physical activities

| 10 | 9 | 8 | 7 | 6 | 5 | 4 | 3 | 2 | 1 |

Music appreciation

| 10 | 9 | 8 | 7 | 6 | 5 | 4 | 3 | 2 | 1 |

Use of literature

| 10 | 9 | 8 | 7 | 6 | 5 | 4 | 3 | 2 | 1 |

Opportunities for verbal expression

| 10 | 9 | 8 | 7 | 6 | 5 | 4 | 3 | 2 | 1 |

Field trips

| 10 | 9 | 8 | 7 | 6 | 5 | 4 | 3 | 2 | 1 |

Use of outside resources

| 10 | 9 | 8 | 7 | 6 | 5 | 4 | 3 | 2 | 1 |

Newsletters

| 10 | 9 | 8 | 7 | 6 | 5 | 4 | 3 | 2 | 1 |

© 1990 by The Center for Applied Research in Education, Inc.

FACILITY

Safe

| 10 | 9 | 8 | 7 | 6 | 5 | 4 | 3 | 2 | 1 |

Child-oriented

| 10 | 9 | 8 | 7 | 6 | 5 | 4 | 3 | 2 | 1 |

Inviting

| 10 | 9 | 8 | 7 | 6 | 5 | 4 | 3 | 2 | 1 |

Attractive

| 10 | 9 | 8 | 7 | 6 | 5 | 4 | 3 | 2 | 1 |

Stimulating

| 10 | 9 | 8 | 7 | 6 | 5 | 4 | 3 | 2 | 1 |

Comfortable

| 10 | 9 | 8 | 7 | 6 | 5 | 4 | 3 | 2 | 1 |

Neat and clean

| 10 | 9 | 8 | 7 | 6 | 5 | 4 | 3 | 2 | 1 |

Accessible

| 10 | 9 | 8 | 7 | 6 | 5 | 4 | 3 | 2 | 1 |

STAFF

Professional

| 10 | 9 | 8 | 7 | 6 | 5 | 4 | 3 | 2 | 1 |

Knowledgeable

| 10 | 9 | 8 | 7 | 6 | 5 | 4 | 3 | 2 | 1 |

Child-oriented

| 10 | 9 | 8 | 7 | 6 | 5 | 4 | 3 | 2 | 1 |

Responsible

| 10 | 9 | 8 | 7 | 6 | 5 | 4 | 3 | 2 | 1 |

Prepared

| 10 | 9 | 8 | 7 | 6 | 5 | 4 | 3 | 2 | 1 |

Warm and caring

| 10 | 9 | 8 | 7 | 6 | 5 | 4 | 3 | 2 | 1 |

Open and communicative

| 10 | 9 | 8 | 7 | 6 | 5 | 4 | 3 | 2 | 1 |

Helpful

| 10 | 9 | 8 | 7 | 6 | 5 | 4 | 3 | 2 | 1 |

FORM 10–16

Neat and clean

    10   9   8   7   6   5   4   3   2   1

Cheerful

    10   9   8   7   6   5   4   3   2   1

Fun

    10   9   8   7   6   5   4   3   2   1

SNACKS/MEALS

Nutritious

    10   9   8   7   6   5   4   3   2   1

Balanced

    10   9   8   7   6   5   4   3   2   1

Tasty

    10   9   8   7   6   5   4   3   2   1

Appealing

    10   9   8   7   6   5   4   3   2   1

Frequency

    10   9   8   7   6   5   4   3   2   1

Generous

    10   9   8   7   6   5   4   3   2   1

New taste experiences

    10   9   8   7   6   5   4   3   2   1

GENERAL

Cost

    10   9   8   7   6   5   4   3   2   1

Registration procedures

    10   9   8   7   6   5   4   3   2   1

Conferences

    10   9   8   7   6   5   4   3   2   1

Information made available to parents

    10   9   8   7   6   5   4   3   2   1

Opportunities for parent involvement

    10   9   8   7   6   5   4   3   2   1

Efficiency of total operation

    10   9   8   7   6   5   4   3   2   1

FORM 10–16

Comments _____